"Drawing on their loving personal experience and insights from research, Sheila and Sheldon Lewis have created effective and enduring guidelines for both parents and children to transform traumatic events while embracing the joys of their life journey together."

—Kenneth R. Pelletier, Ph.D., author of *Sound Mind, Sound Body*
and clinical associate professor of medicine,
Stanford University School of Medicine

"This book will be a lifesaver not only for stressed-out children but for stressed-out parents as well. This immensely wise, compassionate guide could only have been written by parents who have been there, and who love their children very much. The authors know how to help kids find the magic and security of childhood, which every child deserves. A valuable contribution."

—Larry Dossey, M.D., author of *Healing Words*

"This book provides beleaguered parents with something to do when their child is upset and they feel helpless to intervene with their child's explosive anger or anguishing distress. The how-tos are so simple, and yet they work so well because the interventions are presented as games that capture kids' attention, imagination, and interest. One wonders why it has taken so long to have a book like this for parents themselves, since professionals have used these exercises in hospital situations for some time in dealing with special children and children in special situations in which handling stress is central. I think *Stress-Proofing Your Child* will become a part of smart parents' survival kits, providing an aid when love and understanding just aren't enough."

—Jimmie C. Holland, M.D., professor of psychiatry,
Cornell University Medical College

Stress - Proofing Your Child

Mind-Body Exercises to
Enhance Your Child's Health

Sheldon Lewis
&
Sheila Kay Lewis

BANTAM BOOKS
NEW YORK • TORONTO • LONDON • SYDNEY • AUCKLAND

STRESS-PROOFING YOUR CHILD
A Bantam Book / March 1996

Library of Congress Cataloging-in-Publication Data

Lewis, Sheldon.
    Stress-Proofing Your Child : Mind-Body Exercises to Enhance Your
  Child's Health / by Sheldon Lewis and Sheila Kay Lewis.
        p.   cm.
    Includes bibliographical references (p.   ).
    ISBN 0-553-35319-5
    1. Stress in children.   2. Stress management for children.
  3. Mind and body in children.   4. Mind and body in children—
  Problems, exercises, etc.   5. Child rearing.   I. Lewis, Sheila
  Kay.   II. Title.
  BF723.S75L48   1996
  155.4'18—dc20   95-11204
                                                              CIP

Published simultaneously in the United States and Canada

Bantam Books are published by Bantam Books, a division of
Bantam Doubleday Dell Publishing Group, Inc. Its trademark,
consisting of the words "Bantam Books" and the portrayal of a
rooster, is Registered in U.S. Patent and Trademark Office and in
other countries. Marca Registrada. Bantam Books, 1540
Broadway, New York, New York 10036.

PRINTED IN THE UNITED STATES OF AMERICA

FFG   10   9   8   7   6   5   4   3   2   1

To our children, Ezra and Zachary,
and to children everywhere

A *stress-proof child is* . . .

giving, caring, nonabusive, and mature . . .
mature and sure . . .
when you're sure of yourself . . .
a very nice kid . . .
not afraid to do something different when the old way
    doesn't work . . .
a child who can make other people happy . . .
able to stand up for what's right . . .
someone who doesn't hang around with the wrong
    people . . .
not embarrassed by parents or other people . . .
not bored . . .
so cool.

A *stress-proof child has* . . .

parents who help her make her own decisions based on
    some choices . . .
parents who trust him . . .
stress-proof parents . . .
a good heart . . .
inside the heart,
love and respect,
peace . . .
a nice self . . .
an *inner* self.

(children ages six to eleven)

Contents

Introduction

Noise, chaos, paper airplanes, spitballs . . .

Sheila walked into the fourth-grade classroom and noticed that most of the kids were running around shouting, or throwing things playfully at one another—not surprisingly, since their regular teacher was absent. In one corner of the classroom, though, two boys were wrestling—fighting, really. Their faces were red and sweaty, and as one tried to get away, the other climbed on top of him.

"Break it up!" Sheila shouted. The boys either ignored her or couldn't hear her through the din. One girl, Zoe,* was standing calmly in the center of the classroom, observing the hubbub like the eye of the storm. She took a deep breath and walked toward the two boys who were now punching each other, and said, "Hey, you guys, why don't you just relax?"

The boys stopped long enough to argue their position to the would-be mediator. One of them, Willie, said, "He hit me first!" Then the other boy, Luke, said, "Liar! You started it!"

---

* Although the stories included in this book are factual, in many cases—to protect the privacy of the children involved—names and identifying characteristics have been changed. In some instances, a composite has been created, with one child serving as an example of several children with a similar issue, such as children of divorce or home-alone children.

As the boys started in again, Zoe moved nearer to them. "Why do you two have to always do this?" she asked. "Why can't you be nice for a change, instead of having this stupid fight?"

The boys stopped again. "We've been doing some nice stuff with Sheila," she said. "Why don't you listen to her?"

By now, other kids had dropped what they were doing and circled around. Some of them joined in to support Zoe:

"Yeah, break it up!"

"Yeah, Luke, you go over *there*. And Willie, you go on that side."

"Yeah, Willie, sit next to me. Ignore him."

Willie and Luke listened to their friends and separated. You could feel the whole energy in the room calming down. Zoe, who had orchestrated this shift, once again took the leadership role. "Sheila, last time you came, you were teaching us that yoga and breathing stuff. Could you show us some more?"

"Sure," Sheila said, impressed by Zoe's command of the situation.

"OK, everybody," Zoe said. "Sit with your backs straight and don't talk."

As Zoe took her own seat, the rest of the kids followed her instructions, though a few fidgeted. Sheila took over and led them in a breathing exercise, which helped the class settle down even more.

Later, Sheila said, "Thanks, Zoe."

"No big deal," Zoe replied. And for her, it wasn't.

As educators and writers interested in health and human development, we have been thinking for many years about what makes a child—like Zoe—able to withstand life's stresses and even, on occasion, transform a stressful situation into a positive one—a child who seems secure and centered, but is not *self*-centered; who is self-reliant, but not selfish; who has a good influence on others, and gets a lot out of helping them.

And since we became parents, we've engaged this question almost daily, as well as a more practical one: What can we do to help our children—and others—become more resourceful and less stressed out?

After our first son, Ezra, was born in 1980, like many parents we read a number of books and turned to grandparents and other experts for advice. We mastered the basics of child care but had more trouble mastering our own increasing anxiety and fatigue. Countless daily dilemmas—work versus child care, personal time versus family time—began chipping away at the ideal picture of family life. Should Sheila work outside or try to work from home? How would Sheldon find time for family in the midst of his busy work schedule? Suitable work situations did unfold, including a part-time job at a health center close to home for Sheila. We did what families with young children do—we juggled.

We also created family time around activities that relaxed and recharged us. We exercised, listened to music and danced, created art, celebrated holidays, and played with Ezra and his toys. We practiced yoga and meditation, often with Ezra sitting on our laps. We massaged him to help him relax at bedtime. He liked to mimic our exercises and hatha yoga postures.

When Ezra was about two years old, Sheldon took a year's detour from health and medical writing and editing to teach in the theater department at Sarah Lawrence College. He found that many of his acting students, overwhelmed by the stress of campus life, benefited from a brief period of meditation and relaxation at the beginning of class. Meditation helped them let go of the mental distractions they brought with them to class, so that they could be fully present and focused. He also began to experiment with guided imagery, involving mental pictures and sensory exploration, to unlock the imagination and creativity of his students. He was amazed at how quickly and effortlessly students using imagery were able to "find" their character and freely express their emotions.

Sheila was applying her master's training in educational media to designing programs and classes at the holistic health center. There, fascinated by daily observations of the mind-body influence on health, she studied and later assisted in teaching courses in massage, yoga, exercise, and diet planning.

When our second son, Zachary, was born, it was clear that the basic skills of parenting we'd acquired wouldn't be enough, for he was a child with enigmatic developmental delays and special

needs. We took Zachary to many doctors and had consultations with specialists who performed many diagnostic tests, but although he was labeled "Failure to Thrive"—meaning he wasn't growing or developing at a normal rate—none of these experts ever could fully explain why this was so. Yet while continuing to search for a medical explanation, we felt that there must be something *we* could do.

Thus, we began a program of therapies—speech, occupational, and physical—under the direction of professional therapists. Occupational therapy teaches children how to be more efficient in fine motor skills such as using utensils, tying shoelaces, drawing, writing, cutting, sewing, etc. The children's improvement in functional tasks helps them compensate for and in some cases overcome visual, perceptual, motor, or neurologic impairment. Physical therapy deals more with the large-muscle, or gross motor, groups and teaching children how to crawl, walk, sit up, and move in general when a delay or disability is present. Occupational and physical therapies often overlap.

These therapies, as part of an "early intervention" program helped Zachary master practical life skills. He became more autonomous, self-confident, and resilient to the demands placed on him. Many special educators and therapists believe that early intervention improves later chances for academic success, and this has been the case with Zach, a perfectionistic student whose strong motivation helps him meet many challenges.

We learned the exercises while observing his therapists and, under their guidance, were able to implement some of them ourselves between therapy sessions. For example, Bonnie Bainbridge Cohen, a well-known occupational therapist and movement consultant and founder of the School for Body-Mind Centering in Amherst, Massachusetts, suggested we devise obstacle courses in our apartment to help strengthen Zachary's spatial awareness. We enlisted Ezra to set up the obstacles at different levels using stools to climb on, tables to slide under, and mountains of pillows to vault over. This is still a popular activity in our home.

Many children, especially those with special needs, become frustrated when learning a new task. When this would happen

with Zach, we would do deep breathing with him to calm him down.

Research has shown that breathing deeply can help us relax by slowing down the autonomic nervous system, which is involved in our body's response to stress. (For more on how breathing relaxes us, see Chapter 1.)

Many techniques we were using to deal with Zachary's special needs worked well with Ezra, too. Working them in simply and organically to the daily routine kept us all from feeling overwhelmed or overscheduled.

As our journey as parents unfolded, our work with mind-body techniques continued. Sheldon became the director of publications at the Institute for the Advancement of Health, an organization dedicated to the study of mind-body interactions. From this vantage point, and as editor of both the mind-body journal *Advances* and a newsletter, *Mind-Body-Health Digest*, he became familiar with the vastly growing scientific literature on the mind's ability to influence the health of the body. He was struck particularly by the work of health professionals who, after teaching children relaxation and visualization techniques, found improvement in the health and stress levels of the children who used them. And in 1990 Sheldon attended—and reported on—a landmark event: a conference on emotional literacy (sponsored by the Institute for the Advancement of Health and held at Commonweal in Bolinas, California), at which educators and clinicians came together to share their experiences and ideas on social and emotional learning.

Sheila was on a parallel course in education, teaching students and teachers innovative learning techniques to help them do better in school—by improving their research, study, and memorization skills—along with mind-body exercises to help them relax and concentrate more. For example, Sheila guided a class of fourth graders in visualization—mentally picturing themselves performing each task they needed to complete in writing a research paper. The students later reported feeling "less nervous" about writing their papers. The classroom teacher observed that they worked with greater concentration right after the visualization.

We think most parents instinctively know how to help their children: one child likes music, another a round of roughhousing, a third a good talk. However, so many parents are overworked as the demands of daily living soar that they do not have the time to contemplate these differences.

Just as we can impart to our children our personal or spiritual values, a strong sense of self, or a willingness to help others, we can share with them ways to help themselves. Certainly, when our children are ill or severely stressed, we should turn to our health professionals for care. But, as parents we can help each of our children to become "stress-proof" on a daily basis, and provide them with tools to meet the challenges in their lives.

Social scientists, educators, psychologists, and other health professionals continually probe issues of wellness and health versus stress, and positive versus negative thoughts, emotions, and behaviors. Is feeling or acting in a positive way going to increase health and decrease stress? This is a question that has been debated by many professionals. Do positive emotions such as joy keep us healthy, while negative ones such as anger lead to illness and despair? At a 1984 conference, "How Might Positive Emotions Affect Physical Health?," Dr. Rachel Naomi Remen, a transpersonal psychotherapist in Sausalito, California, and assistant professor of community and family medicine at the University of California at San Francisco, eloquently addressed this issue: "Perhaps there is a positive way to feel all emotions. It seems to me that all emotions serve a purpose and are potentially life-affirming. Perhaps it is not so much the emotions themselves as the way we deal with them that either is or is not life-affirming." Remen suggests that the healthy way to deal with emotion is "Get into it, experience it, have done with it, and let go of it," and that "the only bad emotion is a stuck emotion."

Many helping professionals speak of the need to find meaning in times of crisis. This attempt to engage with the crisis or difficulty rather than be entangled by it leads to healing, which means the process of becoming whole—physically, emotionally, spiritually. No matter how wounded or how negative children may feel, their movement toward wholeness is positive.

We should also not confuse "compliance" with "content-

ment." Children are frequently rewarded for being "good," for being "seen and not heard"—that is, for not complaining or showing their true "negative" feelings. Overly cooperative or compliant individuals may also be extremely distressed. It's a lot healthier for children to express their feelings appropriately—and to know that they can express them without being criticized—than to hold them in.

In actuality, a stress-proof child may on occasion appear to be negative. Sometimes it's appropriate to be negative. For instance, when you've suffered an injustice or you've been hurt, rather than deny your true feelings, it is perfectly acceptable to vent your frustration or complain so it does not happen again. What transforms the negative into a positive is the attitude that even though "I've been treated unfairly and I'm angry, I'm going to get through this and I'm going to be OK." The ability to feel what we're feeling, to come to terms with it and move on, is "life-affirming" and health-enhancing.

A stress-proof child, then, recognizes when he's having a hard time, under stress, vulnerable, or when he's just plain "woken up on the wrong side of the bed." He is learning how to ask for help when he needs it and how to go inside to help himself, using such vehicles as the exercises and examples presented in this book. Feeling in control is as important to our kids as it is to us; when we feel out of control, we may feel crazy, depressed, or hopeless about a situation. So do our kids. The Healthgames in this book give our kids ways to take command even in the face of events seemingly beyond their control.

One way to empower ourselves is by taking action. We can't always make ourselves well when we're physically sick, and children can't prevent their parents from getting divorced, having more children, or moving to a new city. They can't choose their teachers or their classmates. But they can learn to control their reactions to such stressful events or circumstances. In Chapter 1, "Stressbusters," we'll discuss a number of stress management and mind-body health techniques that can help our children develop a sense of control. These exercises are primarily geared toward children ages four to twelve, but usually can be adapted for younger or older children.

Not every child will face the trials of divorce, disease, disability, or even death. But chances are great that they or someone with whom they are close will. Well-adjusted children from intact, "happy" families also face the normal stresses of growing up. One parent assured us that she and her husband had "stress-proofed" their children's lives. Then, on further reflection, she added, "But I guess they can't escape what's happening around them." Chapter 2, " 'Stress Is When You're Having a Rough Time,' " and Chapter 3, "Milestones and Millstones: Coping with Trying Times and Growing Pains," survey the minor to major forms of stress children can encounter, and give ways to help support your children in these circumstances. "Getting Help," the final section of Chapter 3, suggests steps you can take to determine if your child needs professional help and ways to find the appropriate health or mental health professional to work with your child.

In Chapter 4, "Discovering the Real Me," we explore ways children can reach the quiet place inside of them, which in many traditions is called the inner self—we call it "The Real Me." Through meditation, they can get in touch with this place so that they can bring its peace into their daily activities.

Kids can use their bodies to unwind and connect (or reconnect) with themselves through movement, dance, exercise, sports, hatha yoga (meditation in motion), touch, and massage. We discuss these approaches in Chapter 5, "Body-Mind Fitness."

Different children weather stress in different ways. Some children adjust well to major upheavals, while others have a hard time with minor changes in routine, such as taking a new bus route to school. Psychologists call children who fare well in adversity, and who meet and match their challenges, "invulnerable," "invincible," or "resilient." Suzanne Ouelette, a social psychologist at the City University of New York, has called this ability to do well in trying times "personality hardiness." In Chapter 6, "Raising a Stress-Proof Child," we'll look at traits that foster hardiness and stress-resistance—and ways to help our children cultivate them.

The hardy child does not stop at "*self*-discovery" or "*self*-improvement." Whereas self-awareness, self-esteem, and self-confidence are wonderful traits, they are not worth much unless

tested in the waters of daily living and interaction with others. Chapter 7, "The Social Connection: Helping Your Child Get Along with Others," picks up where Chapter 6 ends, offering ways for our children to reach beyond themselves to help and befriend others.

In Chapter 8, "Taking a Hero's Journey," we examine the interplay between the images we create and the images that create us, and how in the form of myths, heroes, and role models, these images deeply influence our children and shape their social consciousness. We'll see how as parents we can transform the impact of negative heroes into positive learning experiences for our children.

Some children have particular challenges to endure, including chronic or life-threatening illness, such as asthma, diabetes, or cancer, or a physical, developmental, or learning disability. Many children, including those who are generally in good health, may have to endure a hospital stay for surgery or other treatment. Chapter 9, "Special Situations," looks into mind-body practices that help ease the extra demands of these extraordinary situations.

An epilogue, "Bringing Healthgames Home," follows, with practical tips on how to get started using Healthgames in your life.

We hope that *Stress-Proofing Your Child* offers rather than quick fixes or Band-Aid solutions, lasting ways of breaking out of stress cycles that contribute to the growth and development of kids and parents as *people* in their own right.

We have practiced Healthgames with children in many educational settings, with our own children and their friends. We hope you and your children will use and enjoy them, to bring greater vitality, wellness, and wholeness into your lives.

Sheldon Lewis
Sheila Kay Lewis
New York City

Chapter 1

Stressbusters

"You just think lovely wonderful thoughts and they lift you up in the air."

—Peter Pan

Several years ago, our son Ezra came home from school in a very agitated state. He threw his knapsack on the floor, his face red with anger. He stomped around the living room of our apartment, the muscles of his face pulled tight into a scowl. "That kid!" he shouted. "I can't take that kid anymore." When we asked him what happened, he told us that a classmate who sat behind him constantly taunted him, calling him names and sometimes using obscene language. When Ezra turned to tell the boy to be quiet, the teacher scolded Ezra for turning around and talking.

"We'll talk to your teacher," we said.

"But what do I do about this kid?" he asked in despair. "He keeps bothering me."

"You may not be able to stop him from bothering you," we said. "But maybe you can learn to ignore him."

"*Right,*" he scoffed.

Ezra was in "overdrive." His whole nervous system seemed to be out of whack from this experience. We told him to take a deep breath. He did. "Now take another one," we coaxed.

"What for?" he asked.

"So that you can relax."

"I can't!" he said, tears forming in his eyes again.

"Just do it," we said. He inhaled deeply and exhaled again—defiantly, to show us it wouldn't work.

"Feel better?" we asked. Reluctantly, a small smile began to play on his lips.

"A little."

"One more," we said. Ezra took another deep breath and let it out.

"Okay, now let's try something," we improvised. "Close your eyes and picture yourself sitting under a waterfall in a stream. The water feels fresh and cool. The sky is pale blue. The air is filled with a beautiful fragrance. The waterfall cascades gently down your back. The water just goes down your back and washes away—like water off a duck's back. Just stay there for a while under that waterfall, letting the water wash over you and away." Ezra sat there with his eyes closed for a few minutes. Then he opened them. The lines on his face had softened, and the muscles of his arms and legs looked relaxed.

"How do you feel now?" we asked.

"Good," he said.

"Now let's try a game. It's an acting game. You play yourself, and we'll play this boy who's been bothering you. Tell us some of the things he says to you."

Ezra did. "Now as we yell these things at you, pretend that our words are the water from that waterfall. Don't let the words in and don't react to them. Just breathe and let the words slide off you."

Ezra agreed. For the next few minutes we hurled epithets at him. "Hey, kid. Hey, you. Hey, Ezra! Hey, what's your problem, kid. You're stupid. You're a jerk."

Throughout, Ezra maintained a beatific grin. "This is fun," he said.

The next day, when Ezra arrived home from school, we asked, "How was school?"

"Fine."

"How was that kid today?"

"Oh, he was the same," he answered cheerfully. "But I ignored him."

The little game we played with Ezra was based on techniques,

such as relaxation and imagery, that researchers, health practitioners, and educators have shown can help children and adults to manage their stress. For example, Dr. Karen Olness, director of international child health at Rainbow Babies and Children's Hospital and professor of pediatrics at Case Western Reserve University in Cleveland, has successfully trained children in these and other techniques to regulate their breathing rates, muscle activity, electrodermal activity,* and peripheral skin temperature—all of which can be affected by stress.

BREAKING THE STRESS CYCLE

These techniques are easy for children to learn. Researchers at Northeastern University gave fourth graders a six-week relaxation training program. These children were able to control their heart and breathing rates better than children their age who didn't receive relaxation training. "Whatever we learn as children—whether how to speak a foreign language, how to play baseball, or how to meditate—we carry with us throughout our lives," says Dr. Dean Ornish, director of the Preventive Medicine Research Institute in Sausalito, California, whose pioneering research showed that adults could reverse their heart disease through a program of stress management, diet, and exercise. "Generally we learn these new skills more easily when we're younger. I would personally like to see mind-body techniques taught in school curricula along with other subjects. People may not apply algebra or trigonometry to daily life, but mind-body techniques can be useful throughout one's life."

The particular methods we used with Ezra—relaxation, deep breathing, and imagery—aren't new. In fact, they're ancient. For thousands of years, people all over the world have used them to center and uplift themselves and to attain a higher state of consciousness. More recently they've been called biobehavioral or self-regulation techniques, because we can use them to regulate

---

* That is, small electrical changes in the skin that usually relate to the amount of perspiration, which increase as a person is more excited or distressed, and decrease as one relaxes.

our bodies' responses to stress. They're also called mind-body techniques, because they use mental or psychological methods in an attempt to influence physical processes. And bioengineer Earl Bakken, who invented the pacemaker, has coined the term cyberphysiology, from the Greek *kybernan*, "to steer," or regulate the body.

Stress itself is a potent mind-body phenomenon; it triggers interactions between the brain, nervous system, and endocrine system. To understand how stress influences our children's health (and our own health), and how these mind-body techniques work, it is helpful to know how our bodies react to stress. At the beginning of the twentieth century, Dr. Walter Cannon, chairman of the Department of Physiology of the Harvard Medical School, extracted a substance from the adrenal glands of cats and injected it into other cats. Cannon found that the cats receiving these injections had certain physiological responses: their heart and breathing rates, blood pressure, and the amount of blood flowing to their muscles increased. Cannon concluded that these physical changes prepared an animal to either fight for its life or run away from a life-threatening situation such as the approach of a predator, so he called this the "fight-or-flight response." (This response has also been called the "emergency" response.) The substances Cannon injected into these animals were epinephrine (adrenaline) and norepinephrine (noradrenaline), which are now known as "catecholamines" or "fight-or-flight hormones."

Although these hormones can save our lives when we're running from a burning building, many modern-day stresses are not life-threatening. When we lose our keys, when a child forgets to take a lunch to school, when someone cancels a date or appointment with us at the last minute, we still may activate this emergency response. By continually releasing stress hormones when we don't need them, our bodies go into overdrive: our blood pressure rises, our breathing and heart rates speed up, our blood vessels constrict, and our muscles tense up (scientists call this state "hyperarousal" or "hyperreactivity"). The result can be stress disorders such as high blood pressure, headaches, stomachaches and other digestive problems, and facial, neck, and back pain.

Stress can take its toll on children, too. Stressed children are more vulnerable to the disorders mentioned above as well as behavior problems, learning difficulties, sleep disturbances (including nightmares and bedwetting), skin diseases, infections, and accidents. Pediatrician Robert Haggerty and his colleagues at New York Hospital–Cornell Medical Center found, for example, that a stressful event often precedes children's bacterial throat infections. Research studies suggest that even physical conditions with a genetic basis—like asthma, allergies, and diabetes—can be adversely affected by childhood stress.

According to a study of children's visits to the doctor, 15 percent of all children have symptoms of psychosomatic illness. An additional 5 to 10 percent have behavior problems. This implies that at least 1 out of 5 children could have health problems that may be caused or exacerbated by stress.

Stressed children are at high risk of becoming stressed adults, because we carry the patterns we learn as children into adulthood. Moreover, stress disorders in adults may begin developing in childhood. As Dr. Reed Moskowitz, founder and medical director of the Stress Disorders Clinic at the New York University Medical Center, says, "Stress disorders exist at all ages. The physiological consequences of stress build up over years and decades. The earlier we learn to deal with our stress, the better our health and energy will be as adults." There is increasing scientific evidence, for example, that plaque begins to build up in children's coronary arteries, suggesting that heart disease begins in childhood and progresses throughout the course of one's life. So learning these techniques as children may have lifelong implications for health, quality of life, and longevity.

RELAXATION

Fortunately, by using simple techniques—as Ezra did—we can interrupt or reverse the fight-or-flight response. We do this by activating the opposite response—what Dr. Herbert Benson, a professor at the Harvard Medical School, calls *the relaxation response*. During the relaxation response, Benson and others have

reported, our metabolism, heart and breathing rates, and blood pressure decrease, the blood flow to our muscles becomes more stable, and there are changes in our electrical brain waves (we produce more alpha, theta, and delta waves).

Many techniques evoke this relaxation response, including deep breathing, meditation, hatha yoga, progressive muscle relaxation (tensing and releasing different muscles), and many other spiritual or secular practices. To elicit the relaxation response a technique must have two essential components. One is focusing our attention away from our everyday thoughts toward another object of focus: a word, sound, thought, prayer, or phrase; our breath or muscular activity; or an image. The second component is what Benson calls "the passive disregard of other thoughts," what practitioners of yoga call detachment, or the witness state.

By using relaxation exercises to regulate the stress response, children can learn to cope with frightening situations, such as a trip to the dentist. Researchers at San Diego State University found that children who learned relaxation and coping skills were calmer and more cooperative during dental procedures than children who didn't learn these skills.

Most of us probably aren't aware of how much tension we hold. We go from being wound up, tense, to collapsing into relaxation, slumping into our couch or easy chair. However, if we were to unwind mindfully, a deeper, more beneficial relaxation would occur. We do this by checking our posture and breathing, stretching stiff muscles, and by directing our attention to parts of the body, one at a time, as in the following exercise:

Exercise 1.1   Muscle Relaxation 10 min. Ages 6–12. (Younger children can do parts of it with an adult.)

1. Sit in a comfortable chair or lie down on the floor. Your back should rest gently against the back of the chair or the floor. (If you sit in a chair, your feet should touch the floor, uncrossed. If they don't reach the floor, rest them on a pillow, or lean forward—away from the back of the chair.)
2. Start with the arms and hands. Clench your fists. Tense the

muscles of your arms by tightening them as much as you can. Notice how they feel when they are tight—like a tight rubber band that is about to snap. Now open your hands and wiggle your fingers. Make them feel wiggly like spaghetti. Shake them out. Enjoy the relief, the feeling of relaxation.

3. Move to the legs and feet. Squeeze your toes and your feet like that tight rubber band. Then tighten your calves, knees, backs of knees, thighs, the entire leg. Shake your feet and make your toes wiggle like little fish.

(Younger children can skip the next paragraph and move to the face.)

4. Tighten your trunk, starting with the shoulder sockets, chest, and ribs, and ending with the stomach. Feel the space around your waist, where a belt would be if you were wearing one. Then let your stomach go. Allow the ribs and chest to relax. If you are holding tension in the shoulder sockets, let your arms and shoulders gently roll back into the floor or back of your chair. Take several deep breaths into the stomach until all tension in your trunk is dissolved. Last, let your hip sockets open, turning outward from the center of your body. Feel loose and relaxed like a rubber band that's let all of the tightness go out of it.

5. Wrinkle your forehead. Shut your eyes tightly. Open them. Crinkle your nose and uncrinkle it. Clench your teeth and unclench them. Make funny faces, tightening and releasing different parts of your face. Now relax and notice how you feel.

6. Check if you feel any tension anywhere in your body. Eliminate that tension by tightening and releasing your muscles. If you're lying down, slowly roll to one side and get up. If you're sitting in a chair, rise slowly.

When Sheila works with schoolchildren, she finds that students can redirect their scattered energy by doing even the briefest version of the muscle relaxation. By focusing the students' attention to the physical body, students could later be directed to focus on an academic or creative activity. Muscle relaxation decreases anxiety, tension, and a host of fight-or-flight responses. It can alter the brain wave state (from the hyperaroused beta to the

relaxed, alert alpha), and when coupled with additional techniques such as breathing, brings a dramatic change to the individual and his or her environment.

BREATH POWER

> *When the breathing is disturbed, the mind is disturbed. When the breath is calmed, the mind becomes steady.*
>
> —Hatha Yoga Pradipika

Any parent who has tried to calm down a crying child has immediately felt the connection between the breath and emotions. We say, "Now take a deep breath," and when the child does so, her agitation begins to dissipate. The reverse is also true. When we comfort a sobbing child who is taking short, shallow breaths, her breathing appears to become more regular.

Breathing links the body and the mind. In many traditions, the breath is seen as a gateway to and from the spirit and a bridge between the mind/body and the soul. In Hebrew the word *ruach* means breath as well as "spirit," and *ruach Ha Kodesh* means "holy spirit." In Latin *spiritus* is the word for breath, and in Greek spirit and breath are *pneuma*. In Sanskrit, the ancient language of India, *prana* means "life force," and refers to breath as well as life's vital force or energy. The regulation of prana is central to many yoga techniques. Control of prana, the breath, is seen as the link from the physical body to the subtle body—the realm of our dreams, thoughts, and emotions. So the breath, which keeps us alive, also affects the quality of our living.

Basketball pro Bob Pettit frequently relaxed before shooting a free throw by taking a deep breath and slowly exhaling, and racing car driver Jackie Stewart practiced deep breathing during his races. A Little League baseball coach we know helps his young players calm down when they're at bat by having them breathe deeply. "Step out of the [batter's] box," he shouts if a player has two strikes against him or her. "Now take a deep breath." We can quickly see the batter take a more relaxed stance and focus more easily on the next pitch. Likewise, a child

who feels paralyzed by anxiety during a test may find that taking a few deep breaths and slowly letting them out clears the mind and reduces anxiety.

Here's a simple and refreshing breathing exercise:

Exercise 1.2   Basic Breathing 2–3 min. Ages 5–12.
Goal: To regulate the autonomic nervous system. To relax. To slow down or focus the mind so that feelings can rise to the level of awareness.

1. Sit very comfortably in an armchair or any way that allows your back to remain as straight and tension-free as possible.
2. Put your hands on your chest, with the thumbs touching just at the corner where the top of the arm meets the chest and the middle fingers touching each other in the center of the chest. Breathe as you normally do.
3. Notice when your middle fingers, which are touching, move slightly apart. Exaggerate the movement by breathing very deeply.
4. Small children can visualize this downward movement as a sack of air filling up the chest as they breathe in, and deflating as they breathe out.
5. Repeat this rhythmically for two to three minutes at a time.

We noticed when Zach got upset, he'd breathe too fast and talk too fast. Then we couldn't understand what he was saying, which got him more upset. One day at the height of his distress, we showed him how to take a deep breath and make his belly big like a balloon. Zach did this and began to relax. The more deeply he breathed and the more he relaxed, the easier it became for him to speak clearly. Now he regularly breathes to relax and is fond of telling other children to take deep breaths when they're upset.

The following Basic Breathing variation, Balloon Breathing, is especially useful for a child who is upset or crying. If you can get him to leave his crying or tantruming aside to do the exercise, he'll be able to deal with what upsets him more calmly:

Exercise 1.3   Balloon Breathing ½–1 min. Ages 3–5.

Goal: To introduce breathing as a relaxation or calming technique. To learn the concept of "in" breathing and "out" breathing.

1. Let's pretend there's a balloon in your chest. Fill your lungs when you breathe in through your nose. Feel the lungs let out air when breathing out through your lips.
2. Now we'll do it slowly. Breathe in and be aware of the air flowing into the balloon, filling it so it's bigger and bigger.
3. Breathe out slowly through your lips, so that bit by bit the balloon deflates.
4. Pause to the count of five.
5. Breathe in again, this time filling your lungs with air. Hold for a count of three, imagining each lung is a filled-up balloon.
6. Breathe out with a sigh that comes from the back of the throat. Warm air leaves through lungs, throat, and mouth.
7. Repeat three times, breathing in and out of the lungs, imagining each lung as a filled-up balloon that deflates as you sigh.
8. Stop and feel a new energy in your tummy and chest. All tension has drained away.

Balloon Breathing is great for younger children. As they grow older and more sophisticated, try the Elevator Breathing exercise below. It can be practiced anytime.

Breathing calms the mind and nervous system, as well as the emotions. As we breathe deeply, a corresponding slowing down of thoughts takes place. In fact, the pull of many scattered thoughts lessens its grip and we experience that we are controlling our thoughts rather than that our thoughts are controlling us.

Many advanced athletes, yogis, and singers practice abdominal breathing, which is sometimes called diaphragmatic breathing because it involves the diaphragm, the large sheet of muscle that is attached all around the lower edges of the rib cage. It separates the abdominal organs (intestines, stomach, liver) from the chest organs (heart, lungs, blood vessels).

Unfortunately, most of us don't maximize the use of our brain power, or of our breath power. Ancient Chinese medical texts such as the *Nei Ching*, or *The Yellow Emperor's Classic of Internal*

Medicine, refer to the abdomen as the seat of the will, and say that abdominal breathing strengthens the will and thus the whole character of a person. Although usually when we breathe we expand our lungs, we do breathe from our abdomen in activities such as singing, swimming, or karate.

The diaphragm helps us to expel air from the lungs when we breathe out. When we breathe in, the diaphragm contracts and lowers. If the muscles of the abdominal organs are tight from tension, the diaphragm will not be able to drop very far. If you can relax the muscles, breathing will go deeper instead of remaining shallow.

Exercise 1.4   Elevator Breathing 1 min. Ages 6–11.
Goal: To extend the mastery of Balloon Breathing. To induce relaxation and regulate the autonomic nervous system.

1. Children learn to isolate three areas—head, chest, abdomen—by holding the breath for six, eight, or twelve seconds in each.
2. Start the elevator ride by inhaling through the nose. As you exhale down, feel the breath travel all the way to the basement (base of spine).
3. Inhale again and take the breath up one floor to the navel (abdomen). Exhale.
4. Inhale a third time to the second floor, to the chest. Exhale.
5. Now you can even inhale up into the attic, up your throat and into your cheeks and forehead. Feel your head filling with breath.
6. When you exhale, feel all tension and worries leave your body and go out the elevator door.

IMAGERY

> *Survey the circling stars, as though you yourself were in midcourse with them. Often picture the changing and rechanging dance of the elements. Visions of this kind purge away the dross of our earthbound life.*
>
> —Marcus Aurelius

An old Indian tale tells of a man who sees a rope, becomes terrified, and runs away because he thinks the rope is a snake. We often see a snake in a rope: when we think we're going to be criticized, when we're called into our boss's office, when we imagine something terrible has happened to our children if they're a few minutes late from school, or when we anticipate bad news when the phone rings at an odd hour. Children see snakes in a rope, too: they imagine doing poorly on a test or losing a game, or feel reprimanded when a teacher casts a glance in their direction. Whenever we imagine the worst, we're doing what Dr. Joan Borysenko, cofounder of the Harvard Mind-Body Clinic and author of many books on mind-body health, refers to as "awfulizing" (a term coined by the noted psychologist Albert Ellis).

Making mountains out of molehills—giving too much weight to problems—is a form of awfulizing. Sometimes we begin our day by awfulizing to ourselves. "I can't bear to get up. This is going to be a horrible day."

Kids do this, too: "I know I'm going to have a bad day, because it's Tuesday, my worst day because we don't have recess and I always get a headache. And we'll probably have a pop quiz in math and I don't understand fractions, and I'm going to flunk . . ." Or: "I know it's going to rain today and we're supposed to have a picnic during lunch and it's going to ruin the whole day."

Though not a particularly uplifting activity, awfulizing— along with just plain worrying—is actually a mind-body practice called imagery.

Imagery is the language of the right side of the brain, the "feeling" brain, where we think in symbols and pictures, as opposed to the left side of the brain, which thinks in verbal language and in a logical, rational, and sequential fashion. Images can encompass the size, shape, texture—the "feel"—of a real object. Just by picturing a rose we may smell it, or by visualizing an ice cream cone, we may taste it.

We employ imagery all the time, such as when we visualize how we want to redecorate a room, or when we mentally rehearse a talk we're going to give. Imagery comes naturally to children, because they move in and out of different states of consciousness all the time. When children play imagination

games—"Let's pretend we're soldiers," for instance—they're using imagery.

Our bodies respond to our mental images of disaster as if they were real events. In other words, just by awfulizing, we set off the stress response we described earlier. By anticipating the worst, such as telling ourselves the presentation we're about to make at work or school will "stink"—even though we're really well prepared—we may actually create a self-fulfilling prophecy, because our body is so pent up with stress by the time we actually give the presentation that it's hard to think clearly and do our best.

Rather than letting our imaginations run wild with worries, which makes us more vulnerable to illness, we can use the mind to short-circuit the cycle of awfulizing by replacing these snakes in a rope with comforting and relaxing images, such as the waterfall Ezra pictured.

Imagery uses our imagination and our feeling brain to program—or reprogram—the body, which is why many top athletes use imagery to improve their performances. As Yogi Berra said, "Ninety percent of the game is mental, and the other half is physical."

Golf champion Jack Nicklaus says he always has "a very sharp in-focus picture" of every shot in his mind.

"First I 'see' the ball where I want it to finish, nice and white and sitting up high on bright green grass. Then the scene quickly changes and I 'see' the ball going there: its path, trajectory, and shape, even its behavior on landing. Then there is a sort of fade-out, and the next scene shows me making the kind of swing that will turn the previous images into reality."

Elizabeth Manley, a professional ice-skater who captured a surprise silver medal at the 1988 Winter Olympics, believes that imagery, along with relaxation techniques, were a key to her success. "I had to learn to do a lot of very difficult jumps under pressure," Manley says. "In learning the triple lutz jump, for example, I would stand at the side of the boards, close my eyes, and picture myself doing the jump perfectly in my mind. Nine out of ten times I would successfully do it by preparing this way."

Research studies have corroborated the athletes' testimonies,

by showing that visualizing an athletic activity combined with relaxation can lead to significant improvement in performance. Scientific research also suggests that movements that are rehearsed in our minds through imagery are actually programmed into our muscles. Dr. Richard Suinn, a sports psychologist and head of the Department of Psychology at Colorado State University in Fort Collins, has made recordings of neuromuscular activity (that is, the interplay between nerves and muscles) during imagery practice using a method called electromyography (EMG). Suinn found, for example, that while a skier visualized himself racing downhill, EMG recordings matched the muscle movements expected on such a course.

Educator Shelley Kessler, one of the leaders of the Social and Emotional Learning movement in education, shared with us how she helped her son and his tennis partner prepare for a tournament using relaxation and imagination:

> When my son Ari was fifteen, he and his doubles partner made it to regionals for the first time. They were both very nervous, so in the parking lot I offered to lead them in a relaxation and visualization exercise. They eagerly accepted. I improvised a relaxation exercise, encouraging them to take a deep breath, to focus and come into synchrony with each other. I asked them to picture themselves playing well and gracefully, to see themselves affirming and supporting each other, and smiling after each point they scored. The boys relaxed and played well. (This type of imagery is sometimes called a mental dress rehearsal.)

If we can program the body to perform certain moves by visualizing them, then we can also program our bodies to relax and feel good by transporting our mind to a magical and calming place.

Exercise 1.5   The Garden of Senses 5–8 min. Ages 7–10. *Goal:* To clear the mind and activate the senses. To enhance creativity and concentration.

1. One person reads (or tells) the following to another or to a group. You may play classical or other instrumental music in the background.

2. With your eyes closed and in a comfortable position, imagine that you are walking into a garden that has been sealed off for years. You have been appointed its caretaker.

3. You want to clear it of musty leaves and rotting branches, so you take a rake and all your gardening tools and start to clean. You untangle the overgrowth and cut off dead branches. You look in every corner and set everything right until the garden sparkles. Now you plant new flowers and shrubbery of many unusual textures and vibrant colors.

4. You hear beautiful sounds coming into the garden, humming insects, chirping birds, the sound of a distant waterfall, mostly the sacred throb of deep stillness. From this stillness your other senses become more acute.

5. You smell things sharply, like fresh pine, clean air, perfumelike scents of rose, jasmine, lilac, and other flowers; the earth, like a rich coffee, gives off a pungent smell. A smoky scent wafts through the air. Someone has started a campfire. Imagine tasting all the delicious foods, topped off by your favorite dessert. Your mouth waters.

6. While you enjoy this imaginary feast, run your hands over the bark of the log you are sitting on; reach down and touch the cool, moist soil.

7. You could stay in this garden forever, it gives you so much for a little care. Your sixth sense tells you this garden is perfect, and you can visit it anytime. It blooms inside your creative imagination, which gives birth each day to new seeds and plants.

8. Take a few deep breaths, breathing in the garden's air. Slowly open your eyes. You may take a pencil and draw your garden, or return to your normal activities.

Note: Some children, particularly those with certain learning disabilities, may have trouble seeing mental pictures. Guided imagery works well with these children. Eventually, after seeing the images suggested to them, the children can move on to creating their own imagery.

MEDITATION

Meditation is the practice of going inside to get in touch with our great inner treasure—the peace, love, and strength within each one of us. Through meditation, we can recharge ourselves, gain perspective on trying situations, and, as our kids say, "chill out." We will discuss meditation in Chapter 4.

HATHA YOGA

Hatha yoga is an ancient system that is closely linked to meditation. You could say that hatha yoga is meditation in motion. It is said that ancient meditation masters spontaneously went into hatha yoga poses while deep in meditation. Hatha yoga strengthens the body and focuses the mind. It can help us concentrate, improve our balance, and feel more centered. Hatha yoga incorporates deep breathing, relaxation, meditation, and imagery.

The two hatha yoga poses that follow may seem very simple, yet they can have immediate profound effects. Notice how your mood or state changes after doing them.

Exercise 1.6   The Mountain Pose 1 min.
Ages 5–11.
Goal: To develop concentration. To improve posture and self-awareness.

1. Stand straight. Imagine a mountain. Feel how strong and sturdy the mountain is. Plant your feet on the ground. Then lift your toes up . . . and bring them down. You may place your hands, palms together, in front of your heart.
2. Tighten your calf muscles. Make them firm, like the side of a mountain. Tighten the other muscles of your legs.
3. At the base (bottom) of your spine is the

tailbone. Imagine that you have a tail that extends from your tailbone. Feel it lengthening your spine, making you stand taller.

4. Stand in place. Then slowly stretch your back as you lower your head toward the ground. Breathe in and out rhythmically, allowing both the image of your tail and the breath to lengthen your spine.

5. Take a deep breath into the center of your chest. Feel your chest opening up as you start to rise, head first, to standing position again.

6. Firm your legs again, and feel the changes in your whole spinal column, neck, and head. Allow your shoulders and arms to relax downward and at your sides.

Exercise 1.7 The Tree Pose 1 min. Ages 5–11.

Goal: To develop balance, concentration, centeredness. To strengthen hand-eye coordination.

Note: At first, you may have trouble keeping your balance, but the more you practice this exercise, the more your balance should improve.

1. Stand straight. Focus on a point in front of you. It may be a picture on the wall, a hook, something at eye level.

2. Imagine that your arms are branches of a tree—very strong and still.

3. Draw them up overhead, about three inches apart. Imagine a string lifting you up from the top of your head toward the sky. Concentrate on the string pulling you up.

4. Draw your left foot into your right thigh. Hold still for thirty seconds. Feel the stretch in your thigh.

5. Now gradually lower your left foot to the floor; then draw

right foot into the left thigh. Keep holding your head high, releasing any tension.

6. Gradually lower your right foot to the ground and arms to your sides, and stand straight, both feet on the ground.

For more hatha yoga exercises and discussion of their physical and all-around benefits, see Chapter 5.

We've touched upon some of the most common mind-body techniques—breathing, relaxation, visualization, meditation, and hatha yoga. In the coming chapters, we will learn more about them, as well as about massage, movement exercises that build hardy personalities and social connectedness, on-the-spot de-stressors, and more.

We'll also look at the hows and whys of stress, so we can become aware of the warning signs in our and our children's lives, and thus be better able to intervene wisely and mindfully. In the next two chapters, we will discuss major and minor stresses confronting our children and begin to map out a positive, active approach to meeting stress head-on and using it as a building block to change and growth.

Chapter 2

"Stress Is When You're Having a Rough Time"

"Stress is when you have so much homework that you don't even have time to play."

"Timed math tests is stress."

"Stress is when you get in trouble and it isn't your fault."

"Stress is the school play and you have a big part."

"Stress is when your father's moving halfway across the country, and you're staying here."

"Stress is when I don't see my parents 'cause they're working all the time."

"Stress is my little brother always wanting to play Nintendo games with me, and he can't even make first level."

"Stress is Mom telling me I have to play with my little sister."

"Stress is my parents fighting all the time."

"Stress is divorce—it's the worst thing that could happen to a kid."

"Stress is when your parents want one thing and you want another."

"Stress is when your parents make you do stuff because they say they know what's best for you."

"Stress is getting called a geeky name."

"Stress is when your friends want you to do something you don't want to do, and they're mad at you if you don't do it—but you're mad at yourself if you do."

"Stress is two outs in the ninth inning, and you're up."

"Stress is getting hurt at the end of soccer and it isn't your fault, but you still have to miss the last game of the season 'cause you're injured."

"Stress is when you have your tonsils out, and your throat hurts, and you can't talk, and you have to eat Jell-O and pudding for five days."

"Stress is when you're having a rough time."
"Stress is pressure."
—Children ages six through twelve

"Pressure"—that's how many of the children we interviewed defined stress. Pressure from parents, pressure from friends, pressure in school. Pressure to perform, to succeed, to conform, to grow up.

As parents we worry that our children will have trouble competing in an increasingly high-tech world. To succeed—or even just survive—we want them to learn math, science, economics, and foreign languages. To be "well-rounded," we want them to excel in sports and the arts. According to Tufts University professor David Elkind, who coined the term the "hurried child," although we "hurry" our children through childhood because we want them to keep up with our constantly changing world, we do them a disservice—because hurried children tend to be stressed children.

Parents today push their children as they push themselves—relentlessly. Some parents even push their slightly precocious offspring into programs for the gifted, like the mother who enrolled her son in a "gifted" kindergarten. "I hope there won't be any *really* gifted kids in his class," she confided to a friend. "I wouldn't want him to be left behind."

The demands on children begin at a very early age and never let up. In large cities, such as New York, Chicago, and Washington, D.C., hundreds of preschoolers compete for a small number of places at the more illustrious private nursery schools. At some of these schools children as young as two and three are interviewed and tested.

Younger and younger children feel the pressure to perform. Says Carol Perry, director of counseling at the Trinity School in Manhattan, "The mother of a three- or four-year-old who is being

tested may have anxiety that the child will not get into the school the mother wants. This anxiety is certainly communicated to the child."

Instead of hurrying our children to grow up too fast, we can help them handle the unexpected changes they will encounter in the future as well as the ones they face today. Here are some of the major pressures on today's kids and ways to help them deal with them.

SCHOOL

Tests. Homework. Report cards. Peer pressure. Parent pressure. Teacher pressure. Learning problems. Distractions. Getting into trouble. School can be an enormous source of stress for kids, which in turn can inhibit learning, just as it can have an impact on health.

Too often, kids feel stressed because they perceive they have no control over a situation. The teacher is unfair. The test is too hard. They don't have a second chance, etc. One obvious, yet frequently overlooked, way to empower children in school is to include them in the process of determining what could be done to improve the situation. We discovered this when Ezra was going through a particularly disorganized time—misplacing his homework, forgetting to do assignments, etc.—and his school adviser (what some schools call "homeroom teacher") called to ask us, "What do you think we should do about this? Why don't you both come to the school and the three of us [teacher and parents] come up with a strategy?" Our response was, "Why don't we invite Ezra to this meeting? After all, he's the person in the situation. Maybe he has some ideas about what's going on and how to handle it. Maybe together we can all come up with a plan that works." The teacher agreed, and it seemed that just including Ezra in the process upped his self-confidence and helped resolve the matter.

Another major problem children have in school is that they become anxious about making mistakes ("getting it wrong") or sometimes, conversely, of being too smart (nerdy or geeky), and

then being criticized or made fun of by their teachers, peers, and/or parents. This anxiety keeps them in a state of overdrive, or hyperarousal, which prevents them from learning fully, because learning requires openness, focus, and risk-taking. So children can become caught up in a cycle of stress and school problems.

More and more, educators and researchers are recognizing the diversity of intelligences—abilities and aptitudes—possessed by children as well as adults. Howard Gardner, professor of education at Harvard University, has coined the term "multiple intelligences" and has identified them as: linguistic (verbal) intelligence; mathematical intelligence; interpersonal or social intelligence—that is, the ability to interact and work well with others (these children succeed greatly in public fields, such as business and politics); spatial intelligence—that is, talent in the visual arts, design, or architecture and/or the ability to visualize objects in space as used in cartography or navigation; musical intelligence; bodily-kinesthetic intelligence, as expressed in dance or athletics; and the frequently ignored (at least in our Western culture), intrapersonal or intuitive/introspective intelligence.

Many schools, however, tend to operate on a narrow, test-taking model that relies most heavily on high aptitude in verbal and mathematical intelligences, leaving out many other areas in which children excel. A child who is unusually perceptive, has keen insights about people and relationships, but has trouble reading, or organizing his thoughts in writing, may be considered only an average student, yet his skills may take him far in the grown-up world of work. Conversely, a super A student who is doing ninth-grade algebra in fourth grade, but has difficulty getting along with or working with others, may find that her high test scores don't assure her of great worldly success after college.

As parents, we can be aware of this and provide additional, esteem-building support. There are many ways to do this:

1. Keep lines of communication open with teachers. Let teachers know things about your child, such as "John is very shy, and he's very good in art. Maybe he could paint the scenery for the

play instead of acting in it, which is making him feel very anxious."

2. Affirming our child's special gifts, especially if they aren't being tagged in school, by saying things like "The way you settled that fight between your friends is better than anything I or any psychologist could have done. You are really good at dealing with people stuff." Or: "You are so good at fixing things. A lot of people with this skill become engineers or inventors or mechanics. You could do that. Have you ever thought about it?"

3. Helping a child learn certain skills, such as test-taking skills, that may not be natural to him or her.

4. Use humor. "It's true, to become an astronaut you don't have to be a great speller, but you don't have to be a poor speller, either." Or "I don't think Mozart was picked first on his team, either. Why don't we get a batting practice in over the weekend?"

5. Asking the child to help around the house with skills he or she excels in. In our family, for example, Sheila is not very mechanical. Since the kids were small, Sheila has asked them to program the VCR or help her with a computer task that is out of her league. This not only lets them know that they have something to offer, but also lets them know it's OK not to be good in everything and to ask for help when you need it. The key point here is that all children should learn to build on their strengths and strengthen or compensate for their weaknesses. By knowing our kids well and objectively, we can help them to see themselves more completely for who they are and what they have to offer, and help them avoid buying into the somewhat limited and limiting way their teachers and classmates may see them. Helping them round out the picture of who they are can help prepare our kids for life after school.

"Alpha-state" learning can prevent this cycle of limitation from occurring—or can interrupt it once it has developed. Alpha-state learning takes place when the child is in a heightened yet relaxed state of alertness, with a sense of inner focus, calm, and confidence. Alpha-state learning unlocks creativity and problem-solving, because when the mind is focused and still, then ideas arise from inside of us. As we mentioned in Chapter 1,

alpha state is that same state of "relaxed alertness" top athletes and artists perform in, and relaxation exercises and imagery can induce this state. (So can art, music, drama, and concentration exercises.)

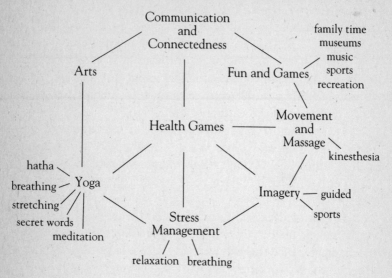

To help families learn to de-stress

Here is an on-the-spot de-stressor, using simple techniques known to induce the alpha state:

Exercise 2.1   **Instant Relaxation** 1–2 min. Ages 7–9.

1. Take a deep breath and let it out.
2. Tell yourself: *Relax*.
3. If you feel yourself starting to get tense or "nervous," just take another deep breath and relax.
4. And if your mind starts to worry or awfulize, don't get involved with those thoughts. Just let them go—like a balloon on a string that you let go of.

Helpful: Learn to recognize your own usual responses to trying circumstances. Where do *you* feel tense? Your back, shoul-

ders, neck, head? Is your throat tightening up? Are you sweating, or do your hands feel cold and clammy?

When you feel these physical changes during class, a test, or while doing homework—or anytime—take a few seconds to calm down. Take a deep breath and let go of the tension, wherever you're holding it. *Remember:* Just taking control of your body's reaction to stress puts you in charge. Even getting into the habit of taking a few deep breaths before a test or before starting homework can help a child do his or her best.

As an educator, Sheila discovered that certain exercises and activities, which we consider to be on-the-spot de-stressors, successfully enhance learning. Working with a group of elementary school teachers over a two-month period, Sheila and a colleague demonstrated a simple approach—which the teachers later introduced to their classes—to help bring the students into the alpha state. Before starting a section on Greek mythology, they began with a few rounds of breathing to classical music. Then they did a visualization in which the students pictured themselves as heroes of Greek myths. After the visualization, they appeared to be more involved in and focused on their work, as they drew pictures and heard dramatic readings of several well-known Greek myths.

In a fifth-grade class, Sheila taught mind-body exercises to help students manage school stress. First, she talked to the class about stress as a physiologic response. Could they feel it in their bodies? Where? Students described the feeling of stress, the physiologic sensations of it, in various ways:

"I feel it in my neck. It's a pain in my neck."

"It's a knot in my stomach."

"It's a red-hot feeling over my face and ears."

Exercise 2.2   Ten-Minute Stretch Break Ages 6–10.
Goal: To unwind as effectively as possible given space or time limitations.

1. Stand tall and straight. Imagine yourself lengthening upward, like a stem growing with a flower blooming on top of it, opening its petals toward the sun.

2. Take a deep breath. If your mind is wandering, focus your gaze on a point or object three to six feet directly in front of you.

3. Raise your arms overhead, touching palms together. Then separate palms and stretch them toward the ceiling. Breathe mindfully as you stretch.

4. Point fingers toward the ceiling or sky as if to touch the stars.

5. Round over, bringing arms toward the floor in a gently stretching motion.

6. Touch the floor with your hands only if you can reach without bending your knees. If you can't reach the floor without bending, place your hands as far down on the backs of your legs as you can, without strain.

7. Rise and now stretch from side to side, with your left arm reaching toward the opposite wall, over your head, then your right arm. Feel a nice opening in your upper arms and shoulders.

8. Sit on the floor, with your legs stretched out in front of you in a V. Leading from the lower back, lean over first your right leg, then your left. Bring your hand to rest on your leg or foot as far as it can without strain. Breathe as you stretch. Try to improve the stretch over each leg three times.

Caution: Never force a stretch. You can do variations on these stretches if there is an injury or space consideration. The important thing is to get all major limbs stretched and opened, from arms to legs to torso. Breathing helps to further the stretch and allows stiff muscles to become more flexible.

In one visit to a third-grade language arts class, Sheila observed the different ways children worked. One group plowed through their spelling and grammar workbook lessons. A second group continually asked the teacher questions, and had a hard time working without her interaction. A few children were unable to sit still long enough to work at all. With the teacher's cooperation, Sheila gave students a choice: to continue what they were doing, or to stop, play some games, and do something special. Some of

the students chose to finish what they were doing and join in later. Sheila helped the others create a different environment. They moved their chairs back away from their desks and sat comfortably in them. A tape of Vivaldi was played softly and the overhead fluorescent lights were dimmed. Then she led them in the exercises that follow, to reinforce what they were learning—in this case, spelling.

Exercise 2.3   The Giraffe 2 min. Ages 6–8.

1. Close your eyes. (*Note*: Young children may find it difficult to close their eyes. It's fine if they do these exercises with their eyes open.)
2. Take a moment to breathe and feel relaxed.
3. Bring your chin toward your chest. Rotate your chin and neck to the right, then the left. Do this for three rounds. Now do a neck roll, rotating the neck all around.
4. Hunch your shoulders up toward your ears, then shrug them down. Do this three times, then hunch up one shoulder at a time for a few rounds.
5. Now sit up as straight and comfortably as you can. Feel your neck getting longer, yet still relaxed. Picture yourself with a long, relaxed neck, like a giraffe's.

Exercise 2.4   The Spelling Game Untimed. Ages 7–9.

1. Close your eyes (optional).
2. Take a moment to breathe and feel relaxed.
3. Imagine a TV screen in your mind. Turn to the spelling station. When you hear a word (said by the leader), see it flash on your screen.
4. The first word is "encyclopedia." See each letter (spell out loud) and then the whole word.
5. Take a snapshot of the word, or trace it in the air as you see it or sound it to yourself.
6. Take a deep breath. The next word is . . . (Repeat the process.)

After the spelling game, most of the students tested each other on the words. Each child was able to either trace, "hear," or visualize the correct spelling of the words.

Even though the students were a bit giggly about closing their eyes and seeing TV screens in their minds, the work period that followed these exercises was very different. Sheila and the classroom teacher observed what we like to call "the quiet hum of alpha": that is, the students concentrated better, questioning the teacher, working with a greater sense of inner purpose, bothering and interrupting others less often. They were freer in the creative drawing and writing activities that completed the language arts lesson.

This was true even of Elvin, a fidgety student who acted as a "blackboard helper" during the Spelling Game. Instead of doing the exercise with the class, he doodled on the blackboard. His teacher later said he had poor reading and writing skills and could not sit still, but that he was so smart, he took everything in. She saw that the relaxation exercises helped him to focus in his own unique way. Afterward, he settled down to work on his own, instead of hopping from table to table as he usually did, checking out what everyone else was doing. Perhaps because his innately strong kinesthetic (bodily) intelligence had been engaged as a blackboard helper, he was later able to concentrate and do his own work.

Poor school performance can be related to children's difficulties in expressing their feelings. Researchers at the University of Washington in Seattle found that children whose parents handled their own emotions well and taught their children to be aware of their feelings and to express them appropriately scored higher on math and reading achievement tests. They also exhibited fewer behavioral and social problems, longer attention spans, lower levels of stress hormones, and a lower heart rate.

According to John M. Gottman, a psychologist and an author of the study, a key factor in children's ability to learn to manage their emotional responses is "emotional coaching"—the parent helps the child talk about the upset feelings and explore options for dealing with those feelings.

Tests

Tests are a source of pressure, in part because they often seem so arbitrary to kids, who see that even if they have studied they might be asked questions they can't answer. Tests also demand that children use their brains' information retrieval systems in a limited time frame, and some children are not as comfortable doing this.

Test anxiety can interfere with a child's ability to answer a question she knows the answer to, and the time pressure of the test can lead certain children to make careless mistakes. Tests are also a common cause of awfulizing for children—having a spiral of thoughts like "I didn't study enough, I don't know the right answers, I'm going to get a bad grade." One anxiety leads to another, and pretty soon the child is so caught up in awfulizing that she or he can barely concentrate on the test. Here is a variation of the exercise above to do before a test:

Exercise 2.5   De-stress the Test Ages 8–10.

1. Take a deep breath and let it out.
2. Tell yourself: *I'm going to do my best.*
3. If you feel yourself getting tense during the test, or if you start to awfulize, just take another deep breath and "breathe out" the tension.

We can't promise you'll get the highest grade, but you should be in a better position to do your best.

Instead of awfulizing, try what we call "awesomizing"—replacing worry and self-criticism with statements of self-confidence, encouragement, and empowerment. Positive-thinking advocates call this approach "affirmation"—that is, affirming oneself and one's actions with statements such as "I am doing well." Sports psychologists call it "positive self-talk"—"I can do better" to turn around a failure, or even simply "Yes!" to celebrate success. We frequently see tennis players talking to themselves both after scoring an important point and after a miss. And when a baseball player strikes out, teammates often

say, "Next time!" by way of support. These are great ways of awesomizing.

Exercise 2.6   Awesomizing Untimed. Ages 8–11.

1. Become aware of how you speak to yourself when you are awfulizing.
2. Catch yourself saying "I can't," "I won't," or "I don't" statements.
3. Reframe these into "I can," "I will," or "I do" statements.
4. One way to do this right now is to write down four awfulizing sentences, and then change them to awesomizing sentences. For example: "I won't get more than a B on my English test, because my teacher doesn't like me. So I may as well not even try," can become "I will work very hard to do my best." In this example, we are not focusing on "so I can get an A," but on the child taking responsibility not to be victimized by his own awfulizing. Of course, we can awesomize in any situation.

The following exercise, Thought Bubbles, is another approach for turning around our attitudes. Try it by yourself, and/or with your child, focusing on one particular problem or issue:

Exercise 2.7   Thought Bubbles Untimed. Ages 8–11.
Goal: To enhance self-esteem. To turn a "negative" thought into a positive step.

1. Sit down with a pencil and paper. Think about a conversation inside your head about something that is bothering you. See how the words in there have a lot to do with how you feel. If you say "I feel rotten," you probably do feel rotten. Think of another thing you could say instead, like "I'll feel better after I take a nap."
2. On a blank sheet of paper, draw a head with "thought bubbles" coming out of each side of the head. Write the words of the first conversation inside your head into the bubble on the left. Write the words of the second conversation into the bubble on the right. It can look like this:

(left)
"I can't do it."
"I refuse to do ——; it's too hard."
"I'll never be good at ——, so why try."
"I can't do my homework with my brother in my room."

(right)
"I haven't learned it yet."
"I'll do it once."
"I'm okay at ——."
"I'll get better at ——."
"I'll put on my headphones to concentrate better when my brother's in my room."

(We'll discuss how our attitudes affect our health in general, and our ability to cope with stress specifically, in greater detail in Chapter 6.)

Homework

Encourage your child to take a few minutes to get centered—through movement, relaxation, or visualization—before launching into homework. Set a timer so that the "getting started" activity doesn't go on too long. One ten-year-old girl shoots baskets for ten minutes into a hoop on her wall. Playing classical music can also help induce the alpha state, and Howard Gardner and other whole-brain-learning advocates believe that the music enhances learning and memorization by balancing the right and left sides of the brain.*

With certain school assignments, such as a term paper, this balance is necessary to accomplish both the right-brain-inspired creative work and the left-brain organizational, logical, and planning tasks.

A fifth-grade language arts teacher asked Sheila to help her students, who were having difficulty organizing their first attempts at writing term papers. Sheila led the class in a round of simple stretches (such as those in the Ten-Minute Stretch Break, above) to release their tension, then guided the whole class in the Steps to Success visualization (below), which helped them

---

* For tapes prepared with this in mind, see the Appendix under "Music."

organize their thoughts and time while also allowing their creativity to flower.

Exercise 2.8   Steps to Success Untimed. Ages 8–12.
Goal: To solve a problem by breaking it down "step by step," or as a "hurdle to jump over" or "ladder to climb." (You may picture the actual specified number of steps—5 steps to get 100 on a test or paper—or just the end result—100 on a test.) To relax around a problem, seeing it as something to master rather than avoid. To teach organizational skills. To locate tension in the body and let it go. To practice using affirmations, or "awesomizing." (We suggest doing the following exercise on paper. Once you have done it a few times and are comfortable with it, you may visualize the steps mentally.)

1. Draw a stairway or ladder on the left side of a blank page. Write on each rung one step that will lead to the top. If the top rung is a finished science report, then the five steps might be about:
   (1) choosing the topic and all the ideas you will cover
   (2) making a list of all your sources, including library books and live interviews
   (3) writing an outline
   (4) writing the report from the outline
   (5) refining the report to a final draft
2. Close your eyes and visualize each step. See the words and a picture symbol of the words, such as "studying at your desk." Keep eyes closed until you see each step clearly.
3. Make a note of any "hurdles" that come up and might interfere with your success, such as finding yourself distracted—thinking about a TV show, for example, or your dislike of something someone said to you. Take a deep breath and let go of these distracting thoughts. (If ideas come up for your project or for other tasks you want to accomplish, write them down.)

I Am ~
Present

I Will ~
Future

STRESS

Jump over the Hurdle

SUCCESS

1. State problem or obstacle.

3. Diagram or draw your visualization on a blank page.

2. Visualize five steps.

Stressbusters ⟶ You can use:

1. Biofeedback   body tells your mind
2. Imagery   your mind tells your body
3. Breathing   connects body/mind
4. Exercise   burns up fatigue
5. Relaxation   let go of tension
6. Yoga   combines 3–5.

Meeting a challenge turns stress into . . . success.

name:

date:

age:

After Sheila led this exercise for the fifth graders, one student, Max, reported excitedly: "At first I didn't want to do this. I didn't really feel any of the stuff anyone else did. But then, as we were doing the visualization, I felt a click go off in my head, like a lightbulb. I saw all these steps, like you described. I wrote them down!"

Max showed the class his wonderful drawing of five steps to success. Since he considered himself "not to be an artist," he was delighted to see that he could create something he never had before.

The two of us have also tried this exercise with adults. In most cases, the adults could visualize steps as well as obstacles. One woman, an attorney named Joyce, was working on visualizing a neat and orderly office. However, she got stuck at visualizing a

specific overstuffed file drawer. After this exercise, she realized she had to tackle this drawer first. In this exercise, we can come in contact with our subconscious blocks, things that get in the way of our accomplishing a task. This is a step to releasing blocks and moving on.

If you're having trouble getting started—picking a topic for an essay, or doing your most creative work, such as writing a story or making an art project—do a relaxation/meditation to clear your mind before you start. You may be surprised at the ideas that come up from inside of you once your mind is quiet. You might also like to add imagery to stimulate your imagination.

The following guided visualization is one Sheldon taught his acting classes to do to increase their focus and help them get in touch with their creativity. Many of his students eventually used this exercise on their own, when preparing for other classes.

Exercise 2.9   Rainbow Imagery 5–7 min. Ages 7–11.
Goal: To release emotional tension. To stimulate the imagination. This works well by itself or after a relaxation exercise.

1. Close your eyes. Feel your eyes looking inside your forehead at the screen of your imagination. See a rainbow on the screen with all the colors you like. For each color, there is a mood or feeling. See each one I describe, or just the ones you want.
2. First, BLUE. Blue can be calm and soothing, like water trickling down your hand. Blue can be free, like the sky. Blue is a good color to see when your body feels very hot. It cools you off like a swim in a lake. What are you feeling while you're thinking of BLUE?
3. Next, RED. Red can give us energy and heat us up. It is good to see if we are cold. Sometimes too much red makes us feel angry. Other times it makes us feel full of love. What are you feeling while you're thinking of RED?
5. YELLOW can make us feel cheerful. It can warm us like the sun and makes us smile inside. If we are sad or lonely, it can brighten our mood. What are you feeling while you're thinking of YELLOW?
6. GREEN is the color of nature. If we are sick or cooped up

inside, seeing green can help us feel better. What are you feeling while you're thinking of GREEN?

You can see how different colors affect moods and even your health. Try to see or use some other colors.

Outside the Classroom

Specialized summer and after-school programs are springing up across the country to help students achieve higher grades and excel.

In SuperCamp, a nationwide, intensive summer program founded by Bobbi DePorter, she and her associates report that during ten-day camplike sessions, students have breakthroughs. The trust-building, creative, and physically challenging exercises facilitate this process, which then carries over to academic areas.

This was the case with Tyson, who took the program one summer and then had great success in school with SLANT, a technique to help you concentrate and pay attention in class. Without increasing his studying time, Tyson became an excellent high school student. SLANT stands for:

S—Sit in the front of the room and sit up in your chair.

L—Lean forward, look interested.

A—Ask questions of your teacher and always clarify for yourself.

N—Nod your head and give the teacher a positive response.

T—Talk to the teacher about anything.

Similarly, in the Quest program at the Dwight School in Manhattan, Dr. Joyce Robinson heads a team of teachers who help students with learning difficulties to study more effectively and improve their grades. Sheila has worked with these students, and finds that using QUEST—Question, Understand, Embark, Study with strategies, and Test—helps focus and de-stress students while they are doing their assignments.

First you question your teacher or yourself about what you have to do, then you ask yourself if you understand it. If you do,

embark or start to do your work. If you don't, ask for help until you do. Then pick a study strategy, such as underlining, creating word cards, tape-recording your ideas for a paper, and so on, and do it. Last, test yourself by having someone else ask you questions or by making up your own review sheet or practice test.

Mind-body exercises like the ones above can help excite children's imaginations and improve their academic performance. The goal of these practices is not to pump more information into children and turn them into learning machines, but to help them become more open and receptive to the tasks at hand. In so doing, they will work more effectively, go beyond limitations, and stretch their creative muscles.

Burnout

Like adults, children can succumb to the chronic, unrelieved stress of having to do well. For example, researchers at Appalachian State University in Boone, North Carolina, found that some gifted children experience burnout, a condition generally found in adults who are constantly under pressure to perform. Burnout symptoms include emotional exhaustion, keeping others at a distance, and a failure to recognize one's own accomplishments.

Intrinsic to burnout is a loss of meaning. Kids who "burn out" in school or other activities have lost their inner connection to these activities. School may have become a place where the child chalks up good grades or other accomplishments. It is important to help your child reconnect to himself, by finding meaning in activities he enjoys and/or by reconnecting to others through group activities and by helping others. (See Chapter 7.)

If your child is "burning out," speak to his or her teachers about giving the children choices of subject matter or special projects that reflect their own interests. Sometimes children get pigeonholed into pursuing only one activity they excel at to the exclusion of all else. Encourage your child to try something totally different, just to keep things interesting. For example, we suggested Ezra, a sports fanatic, take a filmmaking course at the Children's Museum of Manhattan. He cowrote a script for a sci-fi

comedy, acted in the student film, learned about film technology and special effects, and said, "Now, this is my idea of fun!"

If the child has burnout on extracurricular activities, such as sports or performing arts, suggest she continue to pursue the activity for the fun of it, without the pressure of performances or competitions.

A great way to "recharge" when we're feeling burned out is through meditation, such as in this simple exercise. (We will discuss meditation in Chapter 4.)

Exercise 2.10   Meditation on Your Breath Untimed. Ages 6–9.
Note: Children will vary in their ability to sit still for meditation. Begin with three minutes, then build up to ten minutes for those who can sit for longer periods.

1. Sit in a chair or cross-legged on the floor, with your back straight but not stiff. (If you sit in a chair, your feet should touch the floor, uncrossed. If they don't reach the floor, rest them on a pillow, or lean forward—away from the back of the chair.)
2. Close your eyes. (*Note:* Younger children may find it hard to keep their eyes closed for several minutes. It's fine if they open them occasionally.)
3. Take a deep breath and let it out. Now continue to breathe at your normal pace.
4. Pay attention to your breathing. Feel your breath going in and out.
5. If you notice your mind is wandering, bring your attention back to your breath.

"STOP PICKING ON ME!"

A group of third graders were gathered on their classroom floor playing board games before the start of the school day. Sheila had come as a visitor to lead the students in concentration exercises and a writing workshop. Suddenly one of the boys, Lyle, burst out, "They're picking on me!" Four other boys cried, "Oh yeah, *he's*

bothering us. *He* called *us* names." After a discussion in which
each of the boys aired his views, there was a respite for Lyle as the
class began.

Sheila wondered how she could help Lyle to like himself
better, let alone help others to like him. Later that morning, she
tried a series of concentration exercises with the class. In particular, the following exercise seemed to help Lyle and several other
students become more centered and sure of themselves:

Exercise 2.11   The Rock 2 min. Ages 7–9.
Goal: To get in touch with your inner strength. To feel centered.

1. Stand straight, with your feet parallel and just two to
three inches apart.
2. Hold your neck, head, and shoulders straight and free of tension.
3. Rock back and forth on your heels and toes, gradually pushing
your heels into the floor.
4. Rock back on your heels until you feel a slight stretch in the
backs of the calves.
5. Stand like this for several seconds, firming and tightening the
muscles of your legs, abdomen, and chest. Feel as solid and im-
movable as a rock.
6. Have a partner gently push you on the shoulder while you
resist. Tighten against their push.
7. You can stay in this pose as long as you like, and in places like
elevators, buses, or standing on a line.
8. Loosen your stance and walk around. Notice any changes in
how you feel. You might feel more confident that others can't push
you around, for example.

We all know kids who are socially inept. They're the ones
wearing thick glasses that slip down their ever-running noses:
They're pudgy, or tall and gangly. They seem to be strangers in and
to their own bodies. They appear unkempt—maybe the shirt is
half tucked in and half out—or maybe they're overly neat. They
might "talk too much"—without connecting to other people, as if
holding an interior monologue out loud, precluding others from

response. Or they may hardly talk at all, except to wail painfully to a teacher or parent after being teased by classmates, "Stop picking on me!" "Tell them to stop."

The children we are describing suffer from a lack of social skills—what Drs. Stephen Nowicki and Marshall P. Duke, two Atlanta psychologists, describe as dyssemia ("dys" for difficulty and "semes" for signal). Kids with dyssemia are those who have trouble picking up social signals from others, and consequently tend to be left out, teased, and scapegoated by their peers.

Although we certainly feel strongly that no child should be ridiculed or scapegoated, our focus here is on helping to increase the self-esteem of the child who is picked on, helping him to develop social skills for getting along with others, and providing alternative responses to being victimized if others do tease him.

Nowicki and Duke, authors of *Helping the Child Who Doesn't Fit In*, have identified six main components of dyssemia. A child may have trouble with one or several of these:

1. Inability to interpret gestures or body language
2. Misuse or misinterpretation of facial expressions
3. Inappropriate speaking or sound level, saying things too softly or too loudly
4. Poor personal dress or hygiene
5. Inappropriate use of space or touching, such as talking into your face
6. Poor use and sense of time, being out of sync with the pace of life—for example, not knowing how long it takes to a perform a task or even what day it is

The authors suggest many creative and yet exacting solutions. For instance, if a child seems to shout at you from too far or too near, you can have him stand at one end of a six-foot strip of tape. Then you can ask him to talk to various imaginary people (a policeman, a stranger, a friend) and discuss with him if and when to touch these people, or other ways to get their attention. For children who fail to make eye contact (or who have trouble with reading gestures), cut out pictures of faces and

develop a picture dictionary of facial expressions. You can say, "When a person stands like this, slouching, he may not be interested in what you are saying." You can develop an "audio dictionary" with tapes to teach a child how to express emotionality through voice tone.

It will take more than one or two exercises to help a child overcome the social barriers of dyssemia, but the effect of becoming aware of the situation and being willing to follow advice (or consult a professional) can help. However, if no action is taken, a dyssemic child risks becoming more isolated from and ridiculed by his peers.

A severely dyssemic child may have no friends, and is often blamed by the very children who pick on him for provoking those attacks. Just as a dyslexic child has difficulty reading, a child with dyssemia has difficulty "reading" himself as others do, mastering even the most basic social skills. But having new options for relating to others can turn a child's life around both by empowering that child and by opening up the possibility of fulfilling relationships with others. We also suggest that kids with dyssemia try the approaches to develop mastery and self-esteem discussed in Chapter 6.

"DESIGNER CHILDREN"

Not only do we hurry our children, but in the words of Trinity School's Carol Perry, we also "design" them—by giving them skills in many different areas without helping them experience the joys of childhood. "This is an age of designer children," she says. "No parent wants an average child."

Ways to Help "Unhurry" and "Depressurize" Your Child

1. Before scheduling any after-school activities, ask your child what she really likes to do. Sometimes our kids surprise us. A talented artist who feels compelled to compete all day in school might like to take a noncompetitive cooking or dance class after school. If you think your child has talent in a particular area she

few times. Think of it as a way to warm up your mind *and* your body.

5. *Remember:* What we call nerves, or nervous energy, *are* energy. Your nervous system is gearing up to deliver the extra energy you will need for the performance, whether it's a race, a concert, a play, or whatever. If you feel as though you can't *contain* the energy, gently bob up and down or gently shake out your arms, as many athletes do, before you go out onstage or on the playing field or court.

6. Immerse yourself in what you are doing. Concentration is focus, and focus can put us into the alpha state—that state of relaxation. Once you are immersed in the activity, the nervous feeling will probably go away.

7. If you make a mistake, let it go and move on.

8. When the event is over, take a moment to cool down, if possible, by gently stretching out and/or taking a few deep breaths and letting them out.

9. Give yourself a pat on the back. Celebrate your achievements, and learn from your mistakes.

Like actors, athletes can fall prey to performance anxiety. Some of the great sports figures keep cool under pressure by using mind-body techniques, such as imagery.

Olympic gold medalist Mary Lou Retton says, for example, "As a gymnast, you do a lot of physical working out, but I'd do a lot of mental imagery, too. I'd see myself performing in my head, and it really helped tremendously. I always pictured myself positively. It gave me confidence. It was especially helpful in the Olympics, which were so important to me. I did all the routines in my head the night before competition. Since I usually had trouble on the balance beam, I'd review that in my mind a lot, picturing myself landing straight on the beam."

At the root of performance anxiety are questions like "But what if I fail?" or thoughts like "If I'm not great, so-and-so won't like me anymore." The performance becomes inextricably linked to the child's self-esteem. As the cycle of anxiety/panic attack— and the awfulizing that accompanies it—grows and grows, the child can interrupt this cycle through breathing and other relax-

ation techniques. By totally immersing herself in the task at hand, the child can rekindle the joy of performing, which can be a liberating and enlivening process.

HOME ALONE

Many children find themselves "home alone," like Kevin, the young hero of the immensely popular film of that title. In the movie, Kevin, a totally dependent child who is utterly incapable of taking care of himself, is inadvertently left at home by his parents, who have gone to Europe. In the course of the film, Kevin learns to take care of his own needs—grocery shopping, cooking, and even defending himself and his home against two nefarious (and somewhat dim-witted) burglars. We suspect that one of the reasons the film is so popular is that it resonates with every child's (and adult's) fears and hopes—the fear of abandonment and the hope for self-reliance and competence.

Approximately 7 million "latchkey" children are home alone every day after school and have to fend for themselves until their parents get home from work. Although some child development experts advise waiting until children are eleven or twelve years old before leaving them at home without adult supervision, many parents who cannot find or afford child care for their younger children reluctantly leave them alone. Studies show that some latchkey children thrive on the responsibility of taking care of themselves (and in some cases, their siblings), while others become extremely fearful, resentful, or irresponsible—and some get into danger or serious trouble. The key to success seems to be matching the child's responsibilities to his or her maturity level and temperament. The family can sit down together and figure out what plans and contingencies work best for everybody. Important considerations include:

• Assessing your child's maturity—regardless of age—to be responsible, safe, and sensible enough to spend time at home alone and to fulfill the particular responsibilities required of him or her (such as watching a sibling).

• Evaluating external circumstances, such as neighborhood safety, the availability of neighbors or other adults in case of emergency.

• Setting house rules, primarily for the child's safety, such as going straight home after school unless she gets permission from Mom or Dad; not answering the door; etc. Use your judgment about cooking. It might be best to leave snacks that don't require the use of the oven or microwave.

• Preparing your child: Make sure he or she has a phone list with your number, and those of adult friends or family nearby.

• Considering how much time the child is home alone— children tend to do better in short rather than long stretches— and whether the child is home alone after dark.

• Talking to your child about her feelings about being home alone. Let her know it's OK to express fear, anger, loneliness, boredom, etc.

• Working together to come up with creative solutions to problems with the home-alone arrangement. For example, if the child does not want to be home alone, create a flexible schedule, if possible—perhaps a play date one day a week at a friend's house, maybe one at your house on another day, and an after-school class on another.

• Checking in on your child when you can.

• Setting up rules for siblings who will be home together.

• Leaving notes and treats.

• Giving your child responsibilities, such as setting the table.

Once plans for staying home alone have been set in motion, the family can meet periodically to monitor how it's going. Throughout this process of determining home-alone arrangements, we parents can sharpen our skills of observation and stress detection. Does her behavior seem unusual (for her) in any way? Does she look tense, as if she's carrying too much of a burden on her shoulders? Does she seem lonely or depressed? Has she been complaining of more headaches, stomachaches, or other health problems since she's been staying at home alone?

We can then respond by modifying arrangements as necessary and providing the child with the support he or she needs.

You may find that the many techniques in this chapter open up new ways of dealing with your children and helping them learn to deal with people and events in their own lives. Seeking out a new way of problem-solving is not a sign of weakness but of resourcefulness. And even the most resourceful parent needs a new technique from time to time.

We can even ask our children for advice. "Listen, I don't know what to do when you don't get to bed on time. I'm at my wit's end. What do you suggest we do to make this better for both of us?" is honest and respectful, while inviting the child to work with the parent in creating solutions or change. Children will feel more confident or competent by being included in decisions that affect them. Parents can let go of their authority without giving up their firmness. And that letting go will de-stress everybody.

In the next chapter, we will look at ways children can override the stresses that accompany major and minor events in their lives, as well as the normal growing pains of childhood.

Chapter 3

Milestones and Millstones:
Coping with Trying Times and Growing Pains

"Dear, dear! How queer everything is today. And everything went on just as usual. I wonder if I've changed during the night? Let me think: was I the same when I got up this morning? I almost think I can remember feeling a little different. But if I'm not the same, the next question is, who in the world am I? Ah, that's the great puzzle!"

—from *Alice's Adventures in Wonderland*, by Lewis Carroll

Our children will not grow four feet at the swallow of a pill, or shrink to the size of a doorknob, as Alice did after her journey down the rabbit hole, but they probably will experience some of the confusion Alice describes upon finding herself "changed."

The nature of childhood is growth and change, and change is inherently stressful because it often involves either giving something up (a baby bottle, for example) or meeting and overcoming obstacles (such as a shy child performing in a school play). Moreover, children's lives undergo many changes—such as family moves or their parents' divorce—over which they have no control. This contributes to the sense of powerlessness children often experience.

Few, if any, children will go through life liking all of their teachers and classmates, feeling that they always get a fair shake, or never dealing with conflict. But conflict is an essential part of life. According to psychiatrist Erik Erikson, inherent in each stage of life is a conflict that must be resolved before moving on to the next stage.

Even infants are in a conflict between trust (the feeling that their parents will always take care of them) and mistrust (the fear that they won't be cared for). If this conflict is usually resolved in a positive way, the child emerges with a sense of hope. In early childhood, the struggle between autonomy and dependence·can shape the child's will. During play age, initiative battles guilt, resulting in a strong (or weak) sense of purpose. The school-age conflict is industry versus inferiority, with competence as the goal.

Along with normal stages of conflict, children may experience certain fears at particular stages of development.

In *The Magic Years*, a classic description of the first three years of life, psychoanalyst Selma Fraiberg presents the story of a child named Frankie whose parents decided to give him a model upbringing. Frankie's parents were intent on preventing him from developing the normal fears and neuroses of early childhood. His breast-feeding, weaning, toilet training—even the birth of a sibling—were timed to occur at the scientifically calculated least-stressful stage of his development. His parents expunged all the scary content from fairy tales and nursery rhymes. When his pet bird died, they wasted no time getting a live stand-in to shield him from the reality of death. According to his parents' philosophy, Frankie shouldn't have been afraid of anything. Nevertheless, much to their puzzlement Frankie developed normal childhood fears. Like many two-year-olds, Frankie became frightened that he would be swept down the drain in the bathtub.

Fraiberg's point, of course, is that fear is a normal part of life and a part of normal child development. In fact, a healthy amount of fear is essential to our well-being, because the fear we feel in the face of danger sets in motion our mind's and body's stress response, which makes possible our potentially lifesaving fight or flight.

Although few of us, like Frankie's parents, believe that we can protect our children from fear or stress, we are eager to see

them conquer or outgrow their dragons, overcome their conflicts, and go through their rites of passage as smoothly as possible. At each new stage of their development we've joyously proclaimed that they've reached a milestone. How relieved we were when our child overcame his fears and started acting like a "big boy." Or when, on the first day of nursery school, our Johnny or Jenny strode confidently into the classroom, waving a cheerful good-bye, while other children were clinging to a mother or father who was trying to run off to work. "My kid isn't stressed," we say. "She has lots of friends, does well in school, and is happy at home." Yet how often do we hear from other parents, "I don't understand it. Rachel did so well until she hit third grade. Now she kicks and screams every morning, saying she doesn't want to go to school." Or: "Danny was one of the most popular kids in his class. Now he doesn't seem to have any friends. He's lonely and miserable all the time." Life is filled with twists and turns that can upset the smooth passage from one milestone to the next. Unfortunately, healthy children get sick, stable families break up, prosperous families hit an economic slump, good students have a tough year in school, families move, and loved ones die.

These disruptive and largely inevitable life events can be like millstones around children's necks and can have temporary or long-lasting effects on their health or development. One study found, for example, that sick children were more than three times as likely to have frequent or severe life events in the year prior to their illness as healthy children during the same period—which suggests that life events play a role in children's health.

This finding supports the research of Seattle psychiatrists Thomas H. Holmes and Richard H. Rahe, who found in their work with adults that a large number of major life events—such as the loss of a job, separation or divorce, a death in the family, and even positive events such as getting married—were consistently related to illness. They created a stress scale based on these results. Researchers R. Dean Coddington and J. Stephen Heisel adapted this scale to assess the stress level of children. (*Note:* The chart is arranged according to the frequency of the events. The greater the stress, the higher the points.)

Stress Scale for Children

Different life events produce varying amounts of stress for children—the more points, the greater the stress.

Life events	Preschool Age	Elementary Age	Junior High Age
Beginning nursery school, first grade, or high school	42	46	45
Change to a different school	33	46	52
Birth or adoption of a brother or sister	50	50	50
Brother or sister leaving home	39	36	33
Hospitalization of brother or sister	37	41	44
Death of brother or sister	59	68	71
Change of father's occupation requiring increased absence from home	36	45	42
Loss of job by a parent	23	38	48
Marital separation of parents	74	78	77
Divorce of parents	78	84	84
Hospitalization of parent (serious illness)	51	55	54
Death of a parent	89	91	94
Death of a grandparent	30	38	35
Marriage of parent to stepparent	62	65	63
Jail sentence of parent for 30 days or less	34	44	50
Jail sentence of parent for 1 year or more	67	67	76
Addition of third adult to family (e.g., grandparent)	39	41	34
Change in parents' financial status	21	29	40
Mother beginning to work	47	44	36
Decrease in number of arguments between parents	21	25	29
Increase in number of arguments between parents	44	51	48
Decrease in number of arguments with parents	22	27	29
Increase in number of arguments with parents	39	47	46
Discovery of being an adopted child	33	52	70
Acquiring a visible deformity	52	69	83
Having a visible congenital deformity	39	60	70
Hospitalization of yourself (child)	59	62	59
Change in acceptance by peers	38	51	68
Outstanding personal achievement	23	39	45
Death of a close friend (child's friend)	38	53	65
Failure of a grade in school		57	62
Suspension from school		46	54
Pregnancy in unwed teen-age sister		36	60
Becoming involved with drugs or alcohol		61	70
Becoming a full-fledged member of a church/synagogue		25	28
Not making an extracurricular activity you wanted to be involved in (i.e., athletic team, band)			49
Breaking up with a boyfriend or girlfriend			47
Beginning to date			55
Fathering an unwed pregnancy			76
Unwed pregnancy			95

Used by permission from *Journal of Pediatrics* 83: 119 (1973).

CHILDREN OF DIVORCE

Holly is a nine-year-old girl whose parents separated when she was two years old. Her mother and father have been involved in an acrimonious custody dispute for many years. Both parents constantly bad-mouthed one another in front of Holly and in public. Holly's mother had been awarded custody, and her father was so upset about the custody arrangement that he showed up at Holly's school at dismissal times on several occasions, angrily demanding to see her.

Both her parents' behavior embarrassed Holly and upset her. She began to withdraw and became angry and frustrated with both her parents. At the suggestion of her aunt, who has practiced meditation for many years, Holly began to meditate in the hope of calming herself down. Through meditation, she began to feel more centered within herself, and as a result, was able to get in touch with what *she* wanted—instead of feeling pulled this way and that by her parents. She told both her parents that she wanted them to go into family therapy with her. During one of the therapy sessions, Holly told her parents that she wanted to have more of a say about when she would spend time with them. She told her mother that she loved her very much but that she also wanted to spend more time with her father. She also told her parents how hurtful their behavior toward each other was to her, and asked them to stop fighting.

Both of Holly's parents agreed to Holly's requests, and have been following her lead to cooperate more with one another. Although the tension is by no means totally resolved, Holly has become more outgoing and feels good about herself and her active role in determining her living arrangements.

Family conflict, separation, and divorce can create a spiral of stress for children. First, the two people a child loves most and depends on for emotional stability are at war. A mother who was previously home may have to get a job outside, leaving the children isolated at a time when they need the most support. A lengthy court case may ensue, sometimes including a custody fight—with the child caught in the middle of the battle. Once the divorce is final and

the child has finally adjusted to the new circumstances, one parent (or both) may remarry, forcing the child to adjust to a new stepfamily, perhaps even a new home and a new school, as did Holly. As one nine-year-old boy whose parents are divorced put it, "Divorce is the worst thing that can happen to you in your life."

Three out of five American children will have to adjust to their parents' divorce and a new stepfamily. According to psychologist Judith S. Wallerstein, founder and executive director of the Center for Family in Transition in Corte Madera, California, children from divorced families can suffer from more potent effects of stress than their parents—which often continue into adulthood—because the family structure is an important aspect of a child's development.

Based on her long-term research of children from divorced families, Wallerstein has identified the different stress effects that commonly affect children of different ages:

Preschool children. Because preschoolers commonly fear they will be abandoned, those whose parents divorce frequently cling to the parent who has custody and may have trouble separating from the other parent after visits. They have trouble sleeping through the night and may regress to thumb-sucking, bedwetting, and/or their attachment to a "security blanket" or other object.

Five to eight years old. Feelings of loss, rejection, and guilt preoccupy children from age five to age eight—they often feel that the divorce is somehow their fault, and they have loyalty conflicts. These children cry frequently and have trouble concentrating and achieving in school.

Nine to twelve years old. These preteens also have school problems as well as behavior problems. They are angry at their parents for getting divorced and may feel anxious, grief-stricken, lonely, and powerless. Children of divorce in this age group often complain of physical symptoms, usually headaches or stomachaches, which are classically linked to stress.

Ways to Help Your Child Adjust to Divorce or Separation

1. Both parents should tell the child together about a decision to separate or divorce.
2. Tell your child why you are getting divorced in general

styles can be confusing to children, and it is unrealistic to expect a child who has had the run of the house to suddenly follow a lot of new rules.

3. Some researchers suggest that the child's original parent should handle discipline issues for the first few years of a stepfamily; others believe stepparents should participate to help form a "real" family. Work out with your spouse and children what works best in your family.

Parents who are going through a divorce should not despair about the welfare of the children, even if their kids are having a hard time. Some research suggests that divorcing parents can help buffer the effects of their children's stress through their sensitivity to their children's predicament. For example, researchers at the University of Ottawa reported that among children whose parents had recently separated, those who maintained frequent contact with both of their parents did better in school than those who spent significantly less time with one or both parents because of the separation. One of Judith Wallerstein's most striking findings was that some of the most distressed children at the time of their parents' divorce bounced back and were doing well emotionally ten or fifteen years later. Conversely, some of the children who seemed to initially handle their parents' divorce well were in trouble ten or fifteen years later. So parents should keep a watchful eye on the ones who seem to be doing well.

That it was impossible to predict which children would do well in the long run suggests to us that *all* children going through stressful circumstances should be given emotional support and should be taught coping skills.

Here's an exercise that children can do to help them recognize and release tension in their bodies. It is especially valuable for the children who have a hard time expressing their feelings over such experiences as divorce. It may be followed by talking to your child.

Exercise 3.1   The Wrinkle Game 2–3 min. in front of a mirror. Ages 4–8.
Goal: To release tension in a fun way.

1. Breathe in and out a few times.
2. Smile wide at yourself in the mirror.
3. Starting at the top of your forehead, wrinkle your entire face—the brows, eyes, nose, cheeks.
4. Shrug your shoulders up and down.
5. Make some wrinkly faces, then have your face relax.
6. If a spot feels tense, say the word "soft," and ask it to go soft. Do the same with your neck and shoulders.

Here are more exercises or breaks that can help a child going through the upsets of divorce. In an unfriendly environment, where hostility is expressed by one or both parents, a child might not feel like doing a quieting or relaxing activity, such as meditation. In this case, she might choose to "burn off some steam" by jumping rope, jumping on a trampoline, doing push-ups, or using a punching bag or basketball hoop—indoors or out.

If old enough, he can go outside for a walk down the block or to a safe place (make sure an adult knows where or accompanies the child). He can walk briskly, breathing in and out, run or skip, bike or skate. Or the child can do lightly strenuous chores, such as scrubbing a floor, cleaning a room, or raking leaves. In the evening or at bedtime, the child can do a stress breaker or state changer such as:

Exercise 3.2   Quiet, Breathe, Release 5 min. Ages 6–10.
Goal: To feel more centered and in control.

1. Take yourself to as quiet a place or room as you can. Sit or lie down in a comfortable position.
2. Notice your thoughts. Are they raging like a storm, wandering all over the place? Whatever they are, tell your mind *Be quiet.* You can say, "Now I need to take time for myself. Thoughts, you can go away and come back later."
3. Start three to six rounds of deep breathing. Inhale through the nose, exhale through the mouth. You may count, "Inhale, 2,3,4," and "Exhale, 2,3,4."
4. As you breathe, exhale into any of the areas where you feel tension. Keep breathing until the tension is released.

Exercise 3.3 The Puppet 5 min. Ages 4–7.
Goal: To feel a sense of control in your body, and then in your thoughts.

1. Do you ever feel as if you are a puppet, pulled on strings by other people? Now you can be the puppet and the puppeteer.
2. Start by standing up straight and freezing into puppet position. Become stiff-limbed like Pinocchio. Tense up your shoulders, arms, and fingers (as if they are made of wood).
3. Stiffen your legs and knees and walk stiff-legged. Keep your whole body wooden and tight. Tense your face, neck, and scalp. This you can do by wrinkling and clenching: wrinkle your forehead and clench your jaw.
4. Now, in your puppeteer voice, tell yourself to "release and go soft." You may swing your limbs to loosen them. You may with one hand massage or rub the tight other hand, and then massage your face with gentle fingertips.
5. It's nice to play the Puppet Game with a friend, sibling, or parent when you can. Take turns. One person acts as the stiff puppet, the other the puppeteer, massaging the puppet's tight neck, face, arms, and legs.

In the following exercises, you can use our examples to create your own scripts.

Exercise 3.4 What Should We Do with This Feeling?
5 min. Ages 3–8.
Goal: To learn different ways to express our feelings.

1. When you are upset, angry, sad, or afraid (or have a different feeling), think of different things you could do with the feeling.

Example: When you're angry, you could have a tantrum, yell and scream, or leave the room, or . . .

you could throw your anger in the garbage . . .

or make a pretend angry omelet with imaginary eggs . . .

or make a picture of your anger.

2. Then do what you thought of—for example, make a ball of fear and play catch with it.

When Zach thinks we're acting silly, he says, "Throw your silly disease out the window." When he gets angry, he likes to pretend to make an angry omelet and then throw the omelet away. Once he said, "I will put all my mad feelings in it. I will put in tomato sauce, paprika, and dill." As he "cooked" the omelet, he let go of his feelings of frustration and anger and began to laugh. "This omelet is disgusting," he said. "Who would want to eat it?"

It's amazing how quickly children (or adults) who are stuck in a particular emotion can change their mood, get unstuck, and move on.

MAGICAL JOURNEYS: GUIDED IMAGERY MEDITATIONS

The following journeys offer "positive escapism," stress breaks that allow children to dispel their tension and re-collect their energy. Use these journeys as time out for positive escapism or distraction, but not as avoidance of dealing with what the child needs to do. It is our experience that focusing on the problem or talking about it may not be productive, especially with very young children. Allowing the child to take a magical journey lets her explore her feelings without becoming overwhelmed by them.

These "Magical Journeys" can be done at home or school. They can be followed by a directed art or writing activity. For instance, at home the child might "make an island setting," using sheets, pillows, and toys as props. In school, the "jet plane" might be linked to a geography lesson, or the "forest journey" to the study of ecology or rain forests.

Exercise 3.5   Jet Meditation 3 min. Ages 6–8.
Goal: To overcome fear of limitation and the limited self. To foster confidence and to fine-tune the balance between "freedom" and "self-control."

🌿 1. Assume a "ready" position as a jet plane, arms out-
spread, standing tall. Perhaps you have a special motor
sound you make before taking off. You can make the sound, either
while moving or sitting still and visualizing yourself flying.
2. You are flying! What do you see above you? Below you? What
do you hear as you fly, and how does it smell?
3. How do you feel flying above the clouds? Really feel this
feeling, and take it back down to earth with you. You are now
flying down and landing back on earth.

Next time you're scared, imagine what it feels like to fly
above the clouds. Up, up, and away!

Exercise 3.6 Tropical Island Meditation 3 min. Ages 6–8.
Goal: To create a sense of space, privacy, and connection with
yourself. To develop creative, imaginative powers.

🌿 1. Sit in a comfortable visualization position. You may
close your eyes. See a beautiful, magical island of paradise.
It could be a place you may have once visited or seen in a picture,
or a place that you create.
2. You are the only human on this island. There are animals
and birds and flowers. What sounds do they make? How does it
smell?
3. You are surrounded by clear, clean seashore and waters. What
does the water feel like when you swim in it? What is the weather
like on the island? Take several moments to feel sun and sea.
4. How does it feel to be alone here? Take the feeling with you as
you swim back to this room. Anytime you like, imagine this place.
Feel the peace of a trip to your own private paradise.

Exercise 3.7 Enchanted Forest Meditation 3 min.
Ages 6–8.
Goal: To feel peaceful, get away from worries. For problem-
solving. Visualize your own beautiful place in the forest.

🌿 1. Assume a comfortable visualization position. You may
close your eyes. See inside a forest filled with magnificent

trees, shrubs, and flowers of all kinds. In the center of a thicket of trees is a white stone bench. Sit on it.
2. Observe the sounds and smells around you. Is it cool and earthy? Does the wind carry the scent of pines? What animal sounds come from the trees and sky?
3. Imagine any fairylike creatures in this forest, come to help you in some way. Perhaps they tell you a secret or solve a riddle or make you laugh. Make friends with these forest creatures.
4. How do you feel now? You have a long walk home through this forest of wonder. As you walk, keep seeing, sensing, and talking to your newfound friends. You may take any advice they offer.

BIRTH OF A SIBLING

The birth of a sibling is another classic stressor for children. "Imagine how you would feel if your husband brought home another woman," a pediatrician told a mother we know. "That's how your daughter feels about her brother." Researchers found that after the birth of a second child mothers tended to play less frequently and interact more negatively with the firstborn child. So even when as parents of a newborn second (or third or more) child we may feel overwhelmed and exhausted, we need to be especially attentive to help our older children and guide them through their transition.

Ways to Help Your Child Adjust to a New Sibling

• Make a scrapbook: When Zachary was a baby and needed a lot of attention, Ezra's nursery school teachers worked with him to make a scrapbook about himself, his family, the things he liked to do, etc. Even though most families have different circumstances, the scrapbook is a great way to let an older sibling know he's special.
• If friends and relatives ask what they can bring for a baby gift, remind them to bring something for the older child as well.
• Set aside "special" time at home and "dates" outside be-

tween the older child and each parent. It doesn't have to be a big deal—even taking the older child shopping may be enough. When Zachary was born, we would take turns scheduling "dates" with Ezra—a brief walk, a game of catch in the park, or going out on the way to school or after school for a "treat."

• Give the older child responsibilities he or she can handle. This reinforces his competence in comparison with that of a baby.

• If the older child wants to regress—that is, engage in babyish behaviors to get more attention—give him permission to act like a baby once in a while: play "crying," baby talk, etc. (You can, too.) This may fulfill the child's need to "regress" to get attention. But couple this with an explanation that the babyish behaviors are not appropriate anymore.

• If the regressive behaviors are destructive, let him know why it's a problem and what the consequences are of acting like a baby. Share with him ways you act like a baby—for example, "I act like a baby when I eat foods I'm allergic to, or when I lose my temper." And discuss the consequences of those behaviors and the advantages of behaving more maturely.

• Include the older child in solving the problem. Say, "I understand you want my attention, but I also have to take care of the baby. How can we work this out so that you get Mommy's [or Daddy's] attention and the baby also gets what she needs?" Frequently, children come up with surprising and innovative ways to work out these problems. They may include helping Mom or Dad to bathe or feed the baby. Ezra was "in charge" of getting Zachary's pacifier and washing it off when it fell on the floor.

MOVING

According to some estimates, approximately one-fifth of all American families move every year, 12 million children move to a different house, and 7 million move to a different school system.

Moving to a new community can be one of the most stressful experiences for children. Moves interrupt friendships, and the new kid at school may feel like an outsider. A new school also

means a new curriculum, and a child may be ahead of or behind his or her classmates in certain subjects. Moves can be particularly difficult for children in kindergarten or first grade, because it can interfere with their normal process of separation from their parents by making them more dependent.

Ways to Help Your Child Adjust to a Move

1. Explain why the family is moving.
2. Talk about ways to keep in touch with friends and relatives the child is leaving behind, such as making a holiday trip back home, phone calls, and letters.
3. Make sure to pack or take along the child's favorite toys, dolls, furniture, etc.
4. In your new location, look for activities that would help your child meet new children and pursue his interests, such as Little League, after-school programs, and church/synagogue activities or scouts.
5. Talk to your child's new teachers about any difficulty he is having adjusting to the new community and school, and make them aware of his strengths and special interests.

Try the following visualization during your family's moving transition:

Exercise 3.8   Moving Pictures 5 min. Ages 5–10.
Goal: To visit a place you miss in your memory.

1. Sit comfortably. Take a few deep breaths.
2. Close your eyes. Relax your head, neck, and shoulders.
3. Imagine a favorite place you once visited, like the seashore, your cousin's house in the country, or the zoo.
4. Visualize all the details, such as the pretty shells on the beach, or the penguin house at the zoo.
5. Enjoy these places in your imagination.
6. Now visit the place you are moving to. If you don't know what it looks like, ask your parents. Picture it as best you can.

7. Repeat a positive statement or "affirmation" about going to this place, such as "I'll have many new friends" or "I'll have a bigger room to play in." You can also notice what you don't like: "I'll miss my friends," "I'll miss the playground." It's okay to feel sad and happy at the same time.

8. Open your eyes. You may want to tell your parents or write down a plan for visiting the friends you'll be leaving behind.

One ten-year-old girl drew her grandparents' home in Puerto Rico as a favorite place. She said just visualizing it always made her happy.

PASSELS OF HASSLES

Daily hassles, the minor annoyances of life, can seem as nerve-racking as a major stressful event. For children, hassles may take the form of being late to school, having a spot quiz in math, getting into an argument with friends, not being invited to a classmate's party, or striking out in a baseball game.

Dr. Ian Wickramasekera, director of the Behavioral Medicine Clinic and Stress Disorders Research Laboratory at the Eastern Virginia Medical School, has said of daily hassles, "Sometimes it is not the mountain in front of you but the grain of sand in your shoe that brings you to your knees." Research has shown that the accumulation of daily hassles is strongly linked to physical health problems. Simply put, a molehill of minor hassles can add up to a mountain of stress.

We used to panic every morning when Zach would dawdle while getting dressed. We knew that if he missed his school bus, we'd all be unhappy. We spent more than a few mornings nagging him, rushing him through his teeth-brushing and breakfast, and running him out the front door to his bus. We noticed how tense Zach looked going to school every day and we thought there must be a better way to deal with the morning time crunch. Together with Zach, we made up some "getting ready" games. After Zach saw a show about a magician/illusionist, he made getting ready a game of magic:

He (or we) would shout, "For the next trick, make Zachary's pajama top disappear. Abracadabra! Shh! Shh! One, two, three!" By the count of three, Zach's pajama top was off. Then he did another magic trick to make his T-shirt go on. It was a lot faster, and a heck of a lot more fun, than rushing him to get ready.

Look at some of the hassles your kids face. You and your kids can come up with games that work for your family.

IT CAN BE STRESSFUL TO BE A CHILD

Whether "hurried" or pressured to achieve, passing through a milestone or a millstone, struggling with a slew of daily hassles and the vicissitudes of modern life, or exposed to a serious trauma, our children can benefit from our support. Some of them may require professional help. But on a day-to-day basis, there's a lot that we can do to help them. Instead of trying to shield our children from stress, we can instill in them a strong sense of self and teach them skills to use when "they're having a rough time."

It helps to remember: being a child can be intrinsically stressful.

Stress comes in many forms, whether as a minor hassle or major hurdle. Like homework, it doesn't just go away because we wish it would. We can't shield our children from stress, but we can change our experience of it and can take the charge off it. One mother said she had made a commitment to not letting her stress and anxiety contaminate her children. Instead of yelling when she gets upset, she works hard at centering herself through exercise, watching her breath, or talking things out calmly. She made a conscious choice to do something positive and constructive during the stressful time. As a result, her children rarely fight and often mediate their friends' disputes.

In our house, we like to view stress as an opportunity to grow or make a change. Sometimes it's hard, as when Ezra and Zach both started new schools. When we are feeling stressed or pressured, we talk it out, by saying what's hard and by reminding each other how we coped with a similar situation in the past. "Oh, yes, you had a really hard time with your new teacher last year, too. What did you

do about it then?" Zach likes to sing a song he made up—"I Hate Change!"—when plans change or things go "wrong," creating verses about the "problem." Sometimes Ezra likes to talk about what's troubling him while playing a game like checkers.

In the next chapter we'll explore meditation, which redirects stress and replaces fatigue with fresh insight and energy. Meditation can affect the whole atmosphere as well as our individual states of mind. More than being a practice to do ten minutes a day, it's a positive state that we can carry with us into our day and that our kids can model. From this state, dealing with a millstone or milestone can become a less tedious task and a more playful adventure.

GETTING HELP

Sometimes our best efforts to help our children don't seem to be enough. Children who are having trouble academically, socially, or behaviorally may be in need of professional help.

Highly stressed children may experience symptoms of stress disorders such as migraines or other types of headaches, digestive problems, skin conditions, and pain syndromes. Should your child have any of these symptoms, be sure to have your child's pediatrician or your family physician perform a thorough evaluation of your child's health. (Don't jump to the conclusion that your child has a stress disorder and take him or her to a psychotherapist without a complete medical evaluation. These symptoms may have other organic causes that require other treatment.)

If you suspect that your child has a stress disorder, learning disability, or psychological or behavioral problem, speak with the school psychologist, a learning specialist, or your child's pediatrician to find out how to have the problem evaluated. A complete medical, psychological, and educational evaluation may need to be conducted. Call up and interview over the phone any of the professionals recommended to you.

Parents can use exercises in this book to relieve stress, while embarking on a plan of action that includes comprehensive evaluation and treatment for the child and/or the whole family.

The following types of professionals may be helpful: pediatricians (who have medical degrees and training in child growth and development), child and adolescent psychiatrists (who have medical degrees and training in psychiatry), clinical psychologists (who have doctoral degrees such as a Ph.D., Ed.D., or Psy.D. and practice psychotherapy), behavioral therapists (who may be psychiatrists, psychologists, or other mental health professionals specializing in hypnosis or biofeedback), behavioral/developmental pediatricians, social workers (whose degrees are usually C.S.W. or M.S.W. at the master's level, and who have training in psychiatric social work or family therapy), licensed family therapists (some states recognize MFCC degrees), learning specialists, pediatric neurologists, and holistic practitioners (professionals in such disciplines as homeopathy, nutrition, and bodywork may offer valuable support to the child being treated medically or with psychotherapy).

It's important to remember that some professionals will diagnose and label your child, while others are reluctant to use labels. We have found that, at best, labels are used to describe or identify particular issues or behaviors for the convenience of a common language and for embarking on a course of action, such as finding a suitable educational placement. Clearly, every child has his or her own unique set of strengths and weaknesses that go beyond labels. For example, a "learning-disabled" child may be poor in reading, but brilliant in math.

SIGNS OF STRESS

According to the American Academy of Child and Adolescent Psychiatry, some of the signs that a child needs psychological, psychiatric, or therapeutic intervention include:

For younger children:

1. Marked drop in school performance
2. Increased efforts in school with decreased results
3. Acting out of worry or anxiety, as shown by not wanting to go to school, go to sleep, or participate in normal activities

4. Hyperactivity, fidgeting or constant movement, or lethargy and decreased activity
5. Persistent nightmares
6. Provocative behavior, such as disobedience, defiance of authority figures, aggression (longer than a few months)
7. Frequent outbursts and temper tantrums

For preadolescents and adolescents:

1. Marked change in school performance
2. Abuse of alcohol and/or drugs
3. Marked changes in sleeping or eating habits
4. Frequent complaints of physical ailments
5. Obsession with body weight; disproportionate fear of obesity
6. Opposition to the rights and authority of others, translated to acts of truancy, theft, or vandalism
7. Prolonged depression, accompanied by negativism, pessimism, poor appetite or change in appetite, thoughts or talk of death
8. Frequent outbursts of anger or violence

WHERE TO GO FOR HELP

You may want to contact national organizations such as the American Psychological Association, the American Academy of Child and Adolescent Psychiatry, the American Academy of Pediatrics, the Society for Behavioral Pediatrics (its membership cuts across disciplines to foster child advocacy, education, research, and clinical care in the subspecialty area known as biobehavioral and developmental pediatrics), and others for a referral to a local practitioner.

For diagnosis and referral, local colleges and universities may offer testing and evaluation services in their schools of education or nursing, or in their psychology departments.

For crisis intervention, local school personnel or mental

health agencies should provide immediate counsel and attention. For long-term therapy, "word of mouth" is one of the best sources of referral—the recommendations of friends, relatives, or their personal contacts. It can be reassuring to send your child to a therapist who you've heard was helpful to another child in your community. Pastors and clergymen can also serve as sources for help.

Friends or relatives who are health or mental health professionals may be particularly helpful. Asking for help is the first step toward receiving needed support. You may wish to take advantage of hospital and community settings that offer parent support groups.

Chapter 4

Discovering the Real Me

And the secret garden bloomed and bloomed and every morning revealed new miracles.
—*The Secret Garden*, by Frances Hodgson Burnett

The Secret Garden is one of the great children's classics of transformation and self-discovery. In it, recently orphaned Mistress Mary, transplanted from India to her uncle's remote old English mansion, discovers a garden that's been locked up for a decade. She is drawn to enter it secretly every day and to restore it to vibrant life. The garden is a metaphor for Mary's own transformation from an unpleasant, spoiled girl to the kind Mary who eventually befriends Colin, a sickly and reclusive hypochondriac. She brings him into the garden and he, too, transforms and grows well. Like the weeds in the garden that are uprooted, the children's negative thinking is replaced by positive attitudes: "Circumstances, however, were very kind to her. . . . They began to push her about for her own good . . . there was no room left for the disagreeable thoughts that affected her. . . ." As for Colin, "new beautiful thoughts began to push out the old hideous ones, and life began to come back to him, . . . and strength poured into him like a flood."

Within each of us is a secret place where only we can go. It's the place where our feelings reside. When we eat a delicious ice cream, the joy we feel isn't in the ice cream—it's inside us. It's that same part of us that we get in touch with when we remember something we experienced as a child, like riding a bike for the first time. And when we are overcome by a stillness or peace from

inside ourselves as we watch a magnificent sunset or a breathtaking waterfall, we are in touch with that same special place within us.

In many spiritual traditions, this place—the inner self—is considered to be the core or essence of our being. It is the part of us that never changes, yet it is the source of all growth and all change. When we are in touch with the self, we can summon up our inner strength and fulfill our highest potential. Even as we grow older, we can connect with our child self at four or six or sixteen as easily as we can recall the smell of a rose.

The self is who we really are. All the roles we play in our lives, all our possessions, skills, and achievements, are ephemeral. One moment we are a student, the next moment an ice-skater. We are good at math but terrible in art (or vice versa). We hit a home run yesterday, but today we struck out.

We may be Texans, but next month we could move to Arkansas. We might suddenly switch careers from a math teacher to a lawyer. We may be Debby's sister or brother, but we're also somebody's son or daughter or cousin. We have so many different identities throughout our lives, so how could any of them be the real "us"?

We change our appearance—we can grow our hair longer or cut it shorter, gain or lose weight, wear jeans during the day and change into a tuxedo or evening gown at night—but we're still *us*. Although we do learn and develop and transform throughout our lives, we're the same "me" that we were when we were younger, and we will be the same "me" as we get older. That "real me" is the self.

Like Colin and Mary, our children are not always aware of their own greatness. Yet by discovering their secret place, the garden, Colin and Mary blossomed into joyful, caring young people and left behind their sheltered, lonely existences. In the same way, by becoming aware of *their* secret place, their "real me," our children can learn that they have inner reserves—strength, stillness, hope—that they can tap into whenever they need to.

THE GOD WITHIN

The ancient Greeks called mankind's essential nature *entheos*, meaning the God within. They believed that *entheos* was the

source of our creativity and noble achievement. In the words of the eminent microbiologist Rene Dubos, *entheos* is "the hidden aspect of man's nature, particularly that which motivates him to perform memorable deeds." The word "enthusiasm" is derived from *entheos*.

The Greek meaning of enthusiasm is more akin to "divine madness" than to cheering at a football game. Ideas and acts born of *entheos* are the product not so much of logic and rational thinking as of divine inspiration. As Dubos wrote, "There would be little chance of improving the world if it were not for the faith derived from the god within."

The self, then, is this god within. This inner divine essence is recognized by every great spiritual tradition. Jesus said, "The Kingdom of God dwells within you." St. Augustine wrote, "I, Lord, went wandering like a strayed sheep, seeking Thee with anxious reasoning without, whilst Thou wast within me. I went round the street and squares of the city seeking thee; and I found thee not, because in vain I sought without for him who was within myself."

An epigram from the Ming Dynasty expresses the same principle: "The spirit of man communes with Heaven: the omnipotence of Heaven resides in man. Is the distance between Heaven and man very great?"

In the Jewish mystical tradition of the Kabbala, neither the body, the mind, nor even the soul is considered to be the real me. "The real me is my sense of volition," wrote Rabbi Aryeh Kaplan. "It is the intangible will that impels me to do whatever I decide to do. . . . If the most basic ingredient of the Self is the will, then this must also be connected to the divine will. In this sense, a person's will comes from the spark of the Divine within the person." This "divine spark" within each of us puts us in touch with our inner self. In yoga, this divine spark within us is called Kundalini.

Although this inner self—the "real me"—is always with us, we're not always aware of it. But we have glimpses of it, whenever anything puts us in touch with our inner worth—the love, joy, and peace inside. Music, for example, can be an "asylum," as Ralph Waldo Emerson called it. "It takes us out of the actual and whispers to us dim secrets that startle or wonder as to who we are, and for what, whence and whereto," Emerson wrote.

Nature is also a great way to get in touch with that inner stillness and strength. As mountain climber Richard M. Emerson put it, "To sit there—totally alone at 25,000 feet, surrounded by a still and motionless world of rock and ice and blue-black sky—was satisfying in a very special way. It was not the euphoria of altitude. It was the exhilaration of wilderness."

Euphoria and exhilaration are feelings we often associate with the creative process. The self is considered to be the source of creativity (in Eastern mysticism, for example). As art educator Peter London, in his book *No More Secondhand Art,* writes, "The experience of drawing from within helps us to uncover . . . a companion . . . [who] already resides within our outer form." This companion, London writes, is "our original self."

Young children—who seem particularly connected to their "original self"—produce some of the most astonishing, creative artwork without worrying what others think. We can nurture this creativity in children by resisting the temptation to compare, correct, or criticize original work.

A nursery school director collected hundreds of her young students' paintings, papering her walls with Miro- and Matisse-like fantasies. Their work was magnificent, original and brilliantly colored. She cautioned that if we don't let very young children freely create, they will stop painting and start mimicking: "By age six, they're correcting themselves and comparing whose giraffe looks most like a giraffe. They are starting to think 'this isn't good enough.' By third grade, many children stop painting altogether, except when it's required."

What happens? In part, children's attention is diverted to other learning and developmental tasks, such as reading, writing, and problem-solving. But that pure, spontaneous, magical spark of creativity doesn't go away. It stays with us our whole lives. It's our connection to our spiritual side, which actually makes us feel more alive.

These feelings of aliveness—*entheos,* if you will—are linked in our minds with the feeling of love. Anytime we feel love toward someone we care about, we experience the self as love. Throughout the ages, great stories have taught us that a tremendous power resides within us in the form of love. The wooden puppet Pinoc-

chio becomes a real boy through his love for his father. Similarly, in Margery Williams's children's classic *The Velveteen Rabbit*, a stuffed animal turns into a live rabbit through the love of a child. And in Steven Spielberg's film *E.T.: The Extra-Terrestrial*, eleven-year-old Elliot's love—more powerful than the most sophisticated medical technology—brings E.T. back to life. The self is that place inside of us where this immensely powerful love can be found.

So love, nature, the arts, and many other phenomena can give us a glimpse of the self. The problem is, often these experiences are fleeting. The ice cream melts. The sunset merges into twilight. The music ends. That fantastic feeling we had hitting a home run disappears the next time at bat when we strike out. What we need is a deeper and longer-lasting experience of the self—one that we can carry throughout our lives.

MEDITATION: PATH TO THE SELF

The sages of every tradition have told us that the way to achieve this goal is through meditation. Meditation is the practice of going inside to discover who we are and to rest in the self—the real me.

Protestant religious scholar Howard Thurman describes experiencing the self as a natural result of going to a place of quiet. As a child he spent quiet hours in his rowboat, where, he said, "there would come a moment when beyond the single pulse beat there was a sense of Presence which seemed always to speak to me. My response . . . always had the quality of personal communion. There was no voice. There was no image. There was no vision. There was God." Many years later, as a minister and teacher, he found that spending these moments in quiet led him to profound inspiration from which his sermons and discourses arose.

In his book *Jewish Meditation*, Rabbi Aryeh Kaplan wrote, "Meditation, which is thought directed by will, can bring many benefits. . . . Through meditation, one can control the thought process and learn to think in new ways, thus gaining new and richer mind experiences."

In the late 1970s, eager to learn meditation to attain some peace of mind, we had the good fortune to meet Swami Muktananda, who, as head of the ancient lineage of Siddha Yoga masters, brought Siddha Meditation to the West. A Siddha master is someone who is immersed in the state of the self all the time and can give others a direct experience of that state. We had never before seen anyone so joyous, and in Swami Muktananda's presence we felt this joy well up from inside ourselves. As he wrote in his book *Meditate,* "There are many techniques which are supposed to lead us to God, but of all of these, meditation is the one recognized by all the saints and sages, because only in meditation can we see the inner Self directly."

To Swami Muktananda, this direct experience of the self is the goal of human life. He writes:

> The truth is that the inner Self
> of every human being
> is supremely great and supremely lovable.
> Everything is contained in the Self.
> The creative power of this entire universe
> lies inside every one of us.
> The divine principle which creates and sustains this world
> pulsates within us as our own Self.
> It scintillates in the heart
> and shines through all our senses. . . .
>
> Without the knowledge of the Self,
> knowledge of outer things is like
> a string of zeroes.
> Zeroes are valueless
> until you place a numeral in front of them.
> In the same way, knowledge of the outer world
> may bring you great material benefit,
> but it cannot in itself bring satisfaction. . . .
> Real happiness,
> real fulfillment,
> comes only when you discover the Self.
> To know the Self is the true aim and purpose of human life.

Meditation can bring us many rewards. By sitting quietly and just being aware of what's going on in the present moment, we learn to become more centered, more "easygoing" in the sense of being able to walk away from a fight without getting reactive. By focusing our mind on a word, thought, or image—or simply, our breath—we learn to concentrate on whatever we're doing, whether it's chopping wood, baking a cake, or assembling a model rocket ship. The activity becomes a kind of wakeful meditation. In this way, children can take mini meditation breaks to improve in sports, their studying, and schoolwork.

Enhanced physical health can be another fringe benefit of meditation. Positive effects on health have been reported, for example, by Dr. Joan Borysenko, in her books, including *Minding the Body, Mending the Mind*, and by Dr. Jon Kabat-Zinn, in his book *Full Catastrophe Living*. Meditation, used in conjunction with diet, exercise, hatha yoga, and stress management, is also an important part of Dr. Dean Ornish's program for people with heart disease. And one scientific study suggests that meditation may even give us the mental power to influence our immune systems. Dr. G. Richard Smith, Jr., of the University of Arkansas, and his colleagues found that a longtime meditator could control her immune system's responses (to varicella zoster, the chicken pox virus) at will.

But the major boon of meditation—its true goal—is serenity and well-being. For children, meditation is an easy way to get in touch with their "real me," or spiritual side—the reserves we spoke of earlier. One child who meditates told us that meditation "puts you in touch with the little voice inside that . . . is almost always right." Another said, "It's stillness." And yet another said, "It's cozy and comfortable and warm." The more children (and adults) meditate, the more this "real me" with its many bonuses and benefits becomes available to them.

When he was in eighth grade, Ezra had a big science project to do. Every day he stayed after school to work on it. Then he would come home, have a late dinner, do the rest of his home-work, and go to bed. Finally, after several days of this, Ezra came home looking quite sullen. "I can't take this anymore. I feel like no matter what I do, that teacher doesn't appreciate it!" Ezra shouted, his arm pitched to punch his fist through the wall.

Sheldon said, "Come on, Ezra, you can do other things besides punch the wall. Why don't you go and meditate?"

To Sheldon's amazement, Ezra replied, "Okay." Ezra went into his room, closed the door, turned on some soft music, turned off the light, and sat down on his rug. He emerged from his room about fifteen minutes later, obviously refreshed and surprisingly reasonable.

"She probably just didn't understand what I was trying to do," he said. "I'll talk to her about it tomorrow."

"Can I make a suggestion?" Sheldon ventured.

"I know, I know," Ezra said. "Stay calm when I talk to her. I will." And he did.

This is one of the powerful effects of meditation. When we are in a tense or difficult situation, just by remembering that state or feeling of stillness we had while meditating allows us to act and speak with the equanimity and calm meditators call "detachment."

One of the most common forms of meditation is mantra meditation—that is, using a special word or prayer that has significance to the person who repeats it. Here is a simple meditation using a mantra or secret word.

Exercise 4.1   Secret Word Meditation 3–5 min.* Ages 3–12.

Goal: To create a positive inner state and enhance self-concept.

Sit comfortably in a chair or on the floor. Choose a mantra or secret word of your own or a prayer that you like. It can be in any language. It can also be a word that makes you feel good, like "calm" or "peace." The most important thing is to pick a word that has a special meaning for you.

Close your eyes. Visualize the secret word written on a screen inside your mind. See it flashing and then still. Now repeat it to yourself for a few minutes. You may feel relaxed, energized, or both.

---

* Older children may be able to continue repeating their secret word longer than younger children, and children of all ages may be able to sustain this meditation for longer periods of time through practice. See what works best for your child.

Just as we focused our mind on our secret word, we focus our mind all the time without even realizing it. Obviously, if we didn't focus the mind, we wouldn't get anything done (at least not very well). Haven't we all had the experience of doing a task—whether driving a car, hanging a picture, or chopping vegetables—with such intense, single-minded concentration that the task seemed to get done by itself? It was as if some inner doer within us was working through us and *we weren't even there*. So where were we? In the space of the inner self.

Dancer and choreographer Jacques d'Amboise said he felt "complete detachment" when he was in total command of his dancing. "When you're dancing like that, you seem to be removed," he said. "You can enjoy yourself doing it and watch yourself doing it at the same time."

Many professional athletes meditate regularly to enhance their concentration and to be as detached as possible during their game or competition. Basketball star Bill Walton said, for example, "I try to do some form of meditation every day. . . . The nicest thing about meditation is that it puts your body in harmony with your surroundings. And that can be real helpful, because when you're a professional athlete, your surroundings can get pretty unharmonious."

Pro golfer Jane Blalock says, "I go into the locker room and find a corner by myself and just sit there. I try to achieve a peaceful state of nothingness that will carry over onto the golf course. If I get that feeling of quiet and obliviousness within myself, I feel I can't lose."

The feeling Blalock describes is similar to the soothing feeling evoked when we watch the waves of the ocean or the clouds in the sky. Try these two meditations to allow the feeling of quiet to permeate your being:

Exercise 4.2   The Sky 5 min. Ages 6–10.
Goal: To relax, feel peace, and gain mastery over one's thoughts. To become aware of and let go of distractions.

1. Sit in a chair with your back straight (but not stiff) and your feet touching the floor. If you prefer, you can sit on the

floor with your legs crossed. Close your eyes.

2. Picture a beautiful blue sky. See the clouds moving across the sky. Just watch the clouds going by. If you start to think about anything, let your thoughts go, just like those clouds. And bring your attention back to the sky. The one who is watching the clouds is the watcher inside. The watcher inside is also the one who is watching your thoughts.

3. The watcher inside is very peaceful, very still, and very happy. Feel that peace, that stillness, and that happiness inside you.

4. Now open your eyes. Take your time to sit quietly if you want to or to get up slowly.

Exercise 4.3   The Ocean 5 min. Ages 6–10.
Goal: To relax completely. To master your thoughts as in The Sky.

1. Sit in a chair with your back straight (but not stiff) and your feet touching the floor. If you prefer, you can sit on the floor with your legs crossed. Close your eyes.

2. Picture the ocean. See the waves coming and going, rising and falling. Keep watching the rising and falling of the waves. If you start to think about anything, just watch your thoughts as they come and go like the waves. And bring your attention back to the ocean.

3. As you watch the waves, feel the stillness inside you. Feel how peaceful you are inside. This is your own stillness and peace. You can feel it whenever you want to.

4. Now open your eyes. If you want to, you can sit quietly for a few moments. When you get up, get up slowly.

The sense of "nothingness," "obliviousness," and "harmony" that many athletes, artists, philosophers, and spiritual seekers speak of—of simultaneously being fully present yet not being there at all, of being totally involved yet utterly detached—is a classical experience of the self described by regular meditators. Meditation masters have called this state witness-consciousness or mindfulness. This witness state is the state of the self.

Meditation sounds so simple that some people don't know how to start. "You mean, I can just meditate?" these people say.

The following meditation can help you to just begin. It's also a good one for experienced meditators:

Exercise 4.4 Mind-Screen Meditation 5 min. Ages 8–12.

🌿 1. Sit in a meditation posture (either cross-legged on the floor or sitting in a chair, with your back straight but not rigid, your legs uncrossed, and your feet touching the floor—if your feet don't reach the floor, place a cushion underneath them).
2. Take a few deep breaths—slow inhalations and exhalations through the nose.
3. Picture yourself in a movie theater watching the screen of your mind. Whatever thoughts or images come up, just watch them come up and then let them go. Don't get involved with them. Just watch the thoughts as they come and go.
4. Become aware of who is watching these thoughts. This is the inner witness, the inner self. Remain in this state of the self for a few moments.

A more extended version of the above meditation, which allows you to meet your meditation guide inside, is called The Watcher:

Exercise 4.5 The Watcher 10 min. Ages 8–12.
Goal: To meet your inner guide and witness, who helps you to know yourself better. To facilitate meditation.

What part of you tells you when you're upset but stays calm all the time? Who watches your dreams and tells them to you in the morning when you wake up?

Inside each of us there is a "watcher" who sees everything (even when we sleep) and stays calm. In the Eastern part of the world, the watcher is called the "inner witness" or "witness consciousness." We can contact the "watcher" inside ourselves through the practice of meditation. Set a timer or clock for five minutes. Now you are ready to start meditating:

🌿 1. Sit in a comfortable cross-legged pose on a rug on the floor, or sit in a chair with your legs uncrossed and your feet

touching the floor—if your feet don't reach the floor, place a cushion underneath them.

2. Close your eyes. Take a few deep breaths. Allow your mind to become still as a quiet lake. If your mind is too busy thinking thoughts, that's okay.

3. Take another breath and send the breath to your heart. Sometimes the heart quiets the mind.

4. Listen for a "voice" deep down inside you. Contact the knower, the watcher, your real self. It may feel like love, or like the joy of running into your best friend after not seeing him or her for a long time.

5. Keep watching. Notice any thoughts, but don't hang on to the thoughts. Just allow them to come and go.

6. Stay still like this until the timer goes off. Then gently come out of meditation. Open your eyes. Come slowly out of your meditation pose.

The more we are established in the witness state or this expanded reality, the more centered we can be in the midst of stresses and conflicts. In this way, meditation can be extremely valuable for all ages. Children who have experienced the treasures of meditation—their own "secret garden"—will be better able to cope with and transcend the ups and downs of daily living.

It can be helpful for you and your child to try different approaches to meditation, and to find the style that suits you best. For some, it's focusing on quiet breathing or nonimagistic energy. For others, the scene, the imagery, is key. Some people get into their thoughts, don't want to let them go, and can be directed to watch them without attachment or judgment. Others will become still-minded.

Zachary, for example, liked to zip in and out of meditation at the flick of a light switch. He would turn on soft music before bed, and with one of us, do his own version of the Golden Traveler, a lovely meditation for young children.

Exercise 4.6   The Golden Traveler 5–10 min. Ages 7–12.
Goal: To tap into our inner self so that we can feel peace, joy, and love.

1. Lie down and breathe deeply. If you can't lie down, sit in a chair. Inhale—breathe in—to your chest a golden light. See the light fill your heart, arms, and legs. See your whole body turn into light as you continue to breathe in and out. See yourself becoming radiant, giving off a golden glow of light. Feel yourself becoming lighter and lighter.

2. In the space of your heart, picture a golden ball of light. This is your Golden Traveler. Now see where the Golden Traveler takes you.

3. Golden Traveler can come with you to school, to the ball field, to a new camp or new home, on a bus, in a car or airplane. You can think of the Golden Traveler as energy, peace, joy, strength, and/or light.

"Close your eyes, Zach. Take a deep breath. Calm yourself."

"I am calm."

"Good. Now let's feel a golden energy, a big ball of light, traveling inside us."

"I feel it, in my tummy and in my ears."

"Ears? Okay, let's meditate feeling the energy in our ears and anywhere else inside our whole bodies. Breathe deep and feel the golden energy travel, up and down, and all around."

A few minutes went by.

"Are you done meditating?"

"Yes. My body is sleeping now but my mouth is talking."

"Can you tell me what it felt like, the golden light?"

"Well, I went to space. It was far away."

"Outer space?"

"No, silly. It was the space before I was born. I wasn't in your belly yet."

"Oh?"

"I was a tiny speck of light. I was just a tiny little nothing."

"How did it feel?"

"It felt good. It felt happy."

"Good night, Zach."

"I'm sleeping."

In that twilight moment before sleep when Zachary was just conscious enough to report "I'm sleeping," there was that delicious moment meditators savor—being fully "there" while at the same time *not* being there, being totally immersed in the present but flying off to a timeless time.

Chapter 5

Body-Mind Fitness

"It's not the Shape that matters in exercise—it's the spirit."
—*Pooh's Workout Book*

The feeling or spirit of exercise—feeling just right with and in one's body—is akin to *entheos*, or the God within in the Greek tradition, the *state of the self* enjoyed by yogis, the *alpha state* described by educators and scientists, and what athletes call the *zone*.

Whatever we call it, what we do through physical actions such as exercise and movement, touch and massage, can transform our mental state and help relieve stress and fatigue. We can thus flip the mind-body coin to the body-mind side. Just as seemingly mind-centered practices such as meditation and imagery can quiet the body's response to stress, body-centered activities such as physical exercises or massage can soothe the mind. (We've already seen that physiological practices such as breathing and progressive muscle relaxation can induce feelings of peace and well-being.) Where the body's work ends and the mind takes over is hard to pinpoint, but for thousands of years people have observed that the body influences the mind and vice versa.

THE BODY-MIND

The way we carry ourselves—our posture and movement—throughout our day both reflects and affects our feelings, attitudes,

and moods (and the reverse is true). The tenser our muscles, the more stressed we feel, and vice versa. Thus, movement and posture can both reveal our inner state and change it. Several body-mind systems, such as the Feldenkrais method, the Alexander technique, and Body-Mind Centering have been developed with the goal of integrating body and mind through movement and bodywork.

Dr. Marilyn Howell, a high school teacher in Brookline, Massachusetts, uses the Feldenkrais method, along with guided imagery, relaxation, nutrition, and hatha yoga, in her Body-Mind Research course. Feldenkrais, Howell says, is based on the theory "that directed movement and mental focus lead to reprogramming of the motor cortex of the brain, which in turn may affect the mind and emotions." According to Howell, her Body-Mind Research students have improved their health, expanded their self-awareness, and deepened their appreciation of the world around them. One student summed up his experience of the course as follows:

"I believe in this society we are always trying to be something that we aren't. . . . No one is ever taught to like themselves, so we have a lot of unhappy people walking around. I have learned to like what I have, to be thankful for what I am, and how to change things I can, like a negative attitude or bad posture. Generally I am more self-accepting and therefore . . . more accepting of others around me. I feel better being able to like the people around me instead of always finding something bad in them. It's a happier world for me."

Although newly discovered by today's students, the link between movement and posture on the one hand, and emotions and attitudes on the other, mirrors the writings of movement educator Mabel E. Todd more than forty years ago in her classic book *The Thinking Body*:

> It is profoundly true that we are as much affected in our thinking by our bodily attitudes as our bodily attitudes are affected in the reflection of our mental . . . states.
>
> We should not know what lies in the imagination if expression did not reflect it. Often the body speaks

clearly that which the tongue refuses to utter. . . . Changing the attitudes of the body is one way to change the mental attitudes; conversely, changing the mental attitudes certainly changes the body's.

Scientific research suggests that our body and mind are more integrated than we may think. Dr. Candace B. Pert, former chief of brain biochemistry in the Clinical Neuroscience Branch at the National Institute of Mental Health, has been studying neuropeptides, messenger molecules that carry information from the brain throughout the body. Pert suggests that when we say we feel an emotion in our gut, it may be that the emotion is actually being expressed in our gut through a neuropeptide that is located there at that time. "The more we know about neuropeptides, the harder it is to think in the traditional terms of a mind and a body. It makes more and more sense to speak of a single integrated entity, a 'body-mind,'" she has said. "In the beginning of my work, I matter-of-factly presumed that emotions were in the head or the brain," Pert continues. "Now I would say they are really in the body as well. They are expressed in the body and are part of the body."

KEEPING IN TOUCH

> Of all the magic in the world
> from near and foreign lands,
> the greatest magic to be found,
> is right inside your hands.
>
> —*Little Earth School:*
> *Education, Discovery, Celebration*

The suggestion that the emotions "are expressed in the body and are part of the body" might help explain why touching—or being touched by—another human being can have such a profound emotional impact. Parents naturally touch and hold their children often. It is reassuring to learn that this in and of itself benefits our children, and scientific studies show that touch is critical

to the growth and development of humans and animals. For example, research by Dr. Saul Schanberg and his colleagues at Duke University found that rat pups who were deprived of their mothers' touch did not produce hormones necessary to their growth and development. Dr. Marshall Klaus's famous "Touch Study" at Stanford University demonstrated that touch improved the chances of survival of premature infants.

Studies led by Dr. Tiffany Field, director of the Touch Research Institute at the University of Miami, found that premature infants who are massaged gain more weight and have lower levels of the stress hormone cortisol than preemies who aren't massaged—and their nervous systems mature faster. Massage not only benefits stressed preemies, it also improves babies' sleep patterns and helps those with sleep problems fall asleep more quickly.

In addition to the positive effects of touch on emotional and physical development, touch has another important benefit for children: it is one of the earliest and most significant ways they learn—about themselves, their environment, and others. Not only do we learn through touch; it's also a way of increasing our learning *potential*. In a study at the Touch Research Institute, office workers who received two massages a week solved math problems faster and more accurately—they completed the problems in half the time and made half as many errors—than they did before getting the massages. The massages reduced the office workers' fatigue and anxiety levels and their brain-wave patterns changed, showing that they were more alert after the massages.

You and your child can invent your own massages. For example, we noticed that sometimes Zachary holds tension in his hands, feet, and legs when he wakes up, so together we made up massages. First, we make "jelly cookies" with his hands. We softly knead his hands as if they were dough, and pat his palms with the "jelly filling." Then we make "sandwiches" to help him unclench his tight hands. We pretend each hand is a slice of bread. Zach calls out the "toppings" of his choice and we "spread" them across his palm.

Zachary: "Mustard, mayo, relish, tomatoes, cucumbers, onions, coleslaw, tuna, pickles . . ."

As Zach's hands gradually open and relax, the tension in his

whole body starts to release. He puts his two hands together to make the sandwich and we all pretend to gobble it up.

Note: A massage can be a nurturing and relaxing activity for a child who wants one. However, no child should ever be forced or pressured to be held or massaged.

THE INTELLIGENT BODY

As we've seen, not only do touch and movement invigorate our health and uplift our emotions, they are among the ways in which we learn.

Children start life as voracious kinesthetic learners. They taste and touch surfaces and textures, they learn to crawl, move, walk, and explore in relationship to the space around them. And yet by the time most children reach first or second grade, this fantastic innate sense is somewhat downplayed or repressed. Children are told to "sit still" to do their math or spelling, when they might learn their numbers and letters better by moving.

Touch, movement, and spatial awareness—how to move oneself or an object in space—is called *kinesthetic intelligence* (as we mentioned in Chapter 2). Bodily or kinesthetic intelligence is one of the seven intelligences identified by Howard Gardner of the Harvard Graduate School of Education. Gardner defines it as "the ability to solve problems or to fashion the products using one's whole body, or parts of the body." People with highly developed kinesthetic intelligence may be skilled or professional at any of the following: fixing or building things with their hands, crafts, massage, dentistry, surgery, dance or performance, and athletics.

All children can benefit from developing their kinesthetic intelligence, since movement, athletics, crafts, and fixing things are significant life skills.

Learning by doing characterizes the kinesthetic learners, who excel in hands-on, multisensory learning environments. According to the field of accelerated learning (as founded by Bulgarian scientist Georgi Lozanov), learning takes place best in an

enriched multisensory environment, which affords opportunities for active and passive activities such as doing and listening.

MOVEMENT AND DANCE

Some children find it easier to learn through movement than sitting at their seat. This has been the experience of Livia Vanaver, who along with her husband Bill directs the Vanaver Caravan, an international folk dance troupe. Vanaver travels across the country as a dance consultant in schools, but mostly works with social studies teachers in school districts in upstate New York. She sees dance as a way of helping children express their feelings along a "different avenue of thought."

"Frequently, the children who are labeled *difficult*—those who can't sit at a desk or are acting out—are the ones who excel in what I'm giving them, which is a physical connection to understanding," Vanaver says. "In the area of movement, they often become the stars and good examples or peer leaders for the rest of class. Through this work, they're seen in a different light by their classmates and teachers. The results in terms of self-appreciation and self-esteem are incredible. This happens almost every time I teach."

Lately, Vanaver has encountered a lot of immigrant children who don't yet feel secure in their ethnic identities. Dance is a means of bridging cultural differences for these children. "In Schenectady, there's a growing Afghani community," Vanaver says. "In one class I visited, there was a third-grade Afghani boy who couldn't read. As I was doing a folk dance, he said, 'Oh, that's like the dances we do.' We asked him what these dances looked like, and he showed the class and later brought in music. The kids began to see him differently. The next week, he came in and said, 'I can read.' So in a short time he transformed from a shy, quiet kid who didn't read to someone who was more outgoing and self-assured. His teacher believes that the connection he made with his classmates through the dance—and discovering that he had something to offer—helped him make that leap. That's often what happens."

Dancer/choreographer Amy Pivar sees dance as an educational and therapeutic tool as well as an artistic medium:

"During dance improvisation exercises when someone is in the midst of creating movement, someone else will often come along and add a movement. People can express themselves and be compassionate in ways that words alone inhibit. Movement can touch people in a space where words are not adequate," Pivar says. "You can work through a lot of stress, and other strong emotions through dancing. It is the releasing of emotional energy and transforming it into a creative act. Kids are so direct, they'll dance, or do a move that expresses how they're feeling—that they're angry—and just doing that will help them. In dance, anger can be expressed in a different, more powerful and often astonishingly beautiful way."

Although taking dance in or after school is wonderful, children do not have to wait to take a formal class to express their feelings through movement. The following exercise, a simple obstacle course that can enhance body-mind intelligence and physical coordination, can be done at home:

Exercise 5.1 Obstacle Course 15–20 min. Ages 4–8. Older siblings or children may serve as "leaders."
Goal: To develop self-concept and body awareness. To stimulate imaginative play. To become more cooperative, graceful, and attentive.

Move any fragile or dangerous objects and furniture from a spacious room out of the way. Take chairs, stools, sofa pillows, boxes, climbing toys, etc., and arrange in sculpturelike unit. Our children like to help design the obstacle course. Children may name the unit "castle," "fortress," "haunted house," or anything else they imagine. Add costumes or sound effects, and play!

Here are two more movement exercises that allow children to have fun while teaching them to be considerate about space—theirs and others:

Exercise 5.2 Bodyspace I 10–15 min. Ages 2–6.
This movement activity is nice to do with a toddler or two, at home or in a toddler center or nursery school class.
Goal: To help children understand boundaries and limits, starting with their own bodies. To develop spatial awareness and consideration of other people's space.

🌿 1. Stick masking tape in checkerboard fashion on the floor
(or use string or sticks). Assign different squares to each
child. Put on some music and have them dance only in their
squares. If they push into another child or enter another's square,
they are "out." This reinforces the goal of differentiating one's
space from another's.
2. Next you can play this without the tape, just telling the
children to respect each other's "bodyspace." Have them deliber-
ately and gently bump and then not bump into each other while
dancing to music you can start and stop.

**Exercise 5.3 Body-
space II** 10–15 min.
Ages 6–8.
Goal: Same as I: To further encourage aware-
ness of self as both
separate from others,
and part of a group. To
develop a sense of physi-
cal integrity—that we
are physically separate
from each other, and
should respect the
bodies of others.

Note: Introduce the idea of an invisible bodyspace to older
children. Some people call it an energy field.

🌿 1. Dance or move around to music. Crowd together and
bump into each other. How does it feel?
2. Slow down and move away from each other. How does that feel?
3. (For more than two people) Shape with your bodies a human
mosaic, in which each child blends into an agreed-upon design
(such as "animals boarding Noah's ark" or "circus artists") without
touching anyone else. It's like trying to make a jigsaw puzzle, with
each person being like a piece next to another piece, but without
touching.
    When two children are fighting, say the word "bodyspace,"
as in "John, give your brother bodyspace. Talk about how you feel

instead of hurting him." Over time, this exercise improves awareness of both the helpful and unhelpful ways to use the body's energy.

EXERCISE AND SPORTS

Intense physical activity, such as exercise or sports, may lead to feelings of stillness, shifts of energy and ecstasy similar to those evoked by meditation or relaxation. William Glasser collected accounts from people involved in what he labels "positive addictions," pursuits such as meditation, running, and crafts. Glasser concluded that "a trancelike, transcendental mental state . . . accompanies the addictive exercise. I believe that it is this same state . . . that the exercisers reach indirectly and that the meditators are trying to reach directly."

Similarly, the late Dr. George Sheehan, a running enthusiast, said that after an hour of running, "I see myself . . . as part of the universe. . . . Every fact and instinct and emotion is unlocked and made available to me through some mysterious operation of the brain." Athletes say that when they reach this state—which they call the zone, or flow—everything goes right, they can't miss, and they feel enormously powerful and ecstatic. Brazilian soccer legend Pelé, for instance, says that he felt "a strange calmness" during one game. "It was a type of euphoria; I felt I could run all day without tiring, that I could dribble through any of their team or all of them, that I could almost pass through them physically. I felt I could not be hurt. . . . Perhaps it was merely confidence, but I have felt confident many times without that strange feeling of invincibility."

John Brodie, former quarterback for the San Francisco 49ers, told Michael Murphy, author of *The Psychic Side of Sports*, that sometimes during a game, "time seems to slow way down, in an uncanny way, as if everyone were moving in slow motion. It seems as if I [have] all the time in the world to watch the receivers run their patterns, and yet I know the defensive line is coming at me just as fast as ever."

Tennis champion Billie Jean King said of a perfect shot, "I can almost feel it coming. It usually happens on one of those days when everything is just right, when the crowd is large and enthu-

siastic and my concentration is so perfect it almost seems as though I'm able to transport myself beyond the turmoil on the court to some place of total peace and calm."

But you don't have to be a world-class athlete or a workout addict to reap the benefits of sports or exercise. Researchers have found, for example, that exercise has a short-term tranquilizing effect that can lower anxiety more effectively than the tranquilizing drug meprobamate. According to some studies, light exercise, such as walking or swimming, can reduce anxiety as successfully as vigorous jogging. (*Note:* Anxiety may actually *increase* during the start of a workout, so hang in there.)

Exercise has also been helpful in relieving moderate cases of depression. In one study, for example, women with mild depression were randomly assigned to relaxation training, a jogging program, or no treatment at all. Although women in all three groups became less depressed after ten weeks, the depression of those in the jogging group improved the most. (*Caution:* Consult your physician before beginning any exercise program.)

Movement and exercise help integrate body and mind. The body becomes a window to the mind and spirit, as basketball player Patsy Neal has so eloquently stated:

"There are moments of glory that go beyond the human expectation, beyond the physical and emotional ability of the individual. . . . One stands on the threshold of miracles that one cannot create voluntarily. The power of the moment adds up to a certain amount of religion in the performance. Call it a state of grace, or an act of faith . . . or an act of God. It is there, and the impossible becomes possible. . . . The athlete goes beyond herself; she transcends the natural. She touches a piece of heaven and becomes the recipient of power from an unknown source.

"The power goes beyond that which can be defined as physical or mental. The performance almost becomes a holy place— where a spiritual awakening seems to take place."

HATHA YOGA

Hatha yoga is an excellent vehicle for furthering body-mind-spirit integration. In hatha yoga, the breath is coordinated with physical

postures called asanas. The goals of hatha yoga include stretching and strengthening the body, increasing stamina, regulating the breath and the prana—the vital energy, or life force—and focusing the mind. This intense mental focus turns our attention within ourselves and brings about a meditative state that leads to an experience of the inner self. Yoga literally means unity or union, which signifies our union with the self. Hatha yoga engages children's imaginations through physically expressive and evocative postures, including the mountain, tree, boat, and animal poses such as the cobra, lion, and cat (see below).

Doing a few hatha yoga exercises provides a complete stretch and relaxation workout. Try the mountain, tree, and animal poses together on one day, and the Sun Salute on the next day. Add any of the visualization, meditation, movement, breathing, or other exercises to hatha yoga as you like. (*Note:* It's best to practice these poses under the guidance of an experienced hatha yoga instructor. If you have a medical condition, an injury, or an area of physical weakness, consult your physician before practicing hatha yoga.)

Exercise 5.4 Sun Salute 5–8 min. Ages 9–12.

Goal: To completely activate, stretch, and stimulate the whole body. To regulate breathing.

The Sun Salute is a series of rhythmic movements designed to wake up the body just as the sun wakes up the earth each morning. It stretches every part of the body and activates the breathing. It loosens the muscles and joints. Each movement is synchronized with the breath; inhale when the chest is expanded and exhale when bending forward. These movements are presented here in full. You can start learning them by doing a few a day slowly. Then add a few more and increase your rate of speed. Finally, perform at least three rounds and up to twenty rounds of the Sun Salute upon rising or late in the day as a refresher, to release fatigue and tension.

The twelve movements correspond to twelve positions on the clock.

1. Prayer Position
     Stand with feet parallel, facing forward and slightly apart. Place palms together at the heart. Breathe in, firming backs of legs and thighs, lifting up from the spine. Breathe out.

2. Stretch to the Sun

Breathe in and raise arms overhead, stretching up from the armpits. Tilt palms toward the sun. Feel the upper chest open and expand, like a sunrise expanding inside your chest. Firm the buttocks and thighs.

3. Welcome the Earth
     Breathe in, maintaining firmness of thighs and legs while lifting up from the spine. Breathe out through the mouth while bending forward from the hip joints. Allow the arms to reach forward as far as possible. Hands may touch the floor beside each foot, while keeping knees straight. Allow head to lower and release. Check that you are bending from the hips and not from the waist.

4. Touch the Ground
     Place hands on floor, fingers alongside toes. Bend the knees, then step back with the left foot, resting the left knee on the ground. Flex the toes so the backs of the toes are on the floor. Keep the right foot parallel to the hands.

5. Mountain and Valley
On the exhale, lunge back, bringing the right foot to meet

the left foot. Lift buttocks toward ceiling, feeling a stretch in the lower spine. Body is in the shape of an inverted V.

6. Upward-Facing Dog
     Slowly drop knees to floor and lower chest and chin to floor, between hands. From this position, inhale, rise up, and hold.

7. Downward-Facing Dog
Exhale and come back up

into an upside-down V position. Feel like a dog stretching its whole body from jaw to paw.

8. Touch the Ground

Inhale, bring right foot between hands, and repeat position 4.

9. Tree Hug

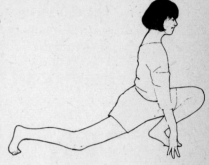

While keeping hands flat on the floor, bring the left foot forward to meet the right foot. Start to straighten up from the legs. Breathe out and lower the torso toward the legs for a deeper stretch. You should be looking at your knees. Hug the backs of your calves or rest your hands on either side of your feet.

10. Tree Swaying in the Breeze

Inhale and extend arms out and up as if they were branches touching the sky. Legs are straight and lifting up so that you feel a slight stretch in the backs of the knees.

11. Tree Resting on Earth

Firmly planted on the earth to greet the morning, you are like a tree. In this, also called the Namaskar, or Prayer Position, feel the sensation of change taking place in your body after this workout. Feel the energy opening up and awakening the space around the joints, the muscles, and the circulation. Exhale softly. You may repeat this.

12. Final Pose

Draw left foot into right thigh and hold for a few seconds.

All of the poses that follow can be used in varied settings, with different goals in mind. For instance, The Cat may be practiced safely at home by a child who is mildly sick. The Lion is a great stress releaser to practice at home or in school. The Cobra

increases flexibility and helps the child who is stiff or sore after an athletic game.

Poses 5–7 introduce hatha yoga in a playful way. Children have fun while their whole bodies benefit.

Exercise 5.5   The Cat 2 min. Ages 6–12.

Goal: To develop the flexibility of a cat. This is a good overall body stretch, especially for the back.

1. Come to a kneeling position on the floor, sitting back on your heels with your arms stretched out in front of you. With your back sloping downward (lowest point is shoulders), lift your neck slightly. This is the resting cat.

2. Inhale, arching your back up, like a scaredy-cat. Bring your chin into your chest. Hold for ten seconds, then exhale down.
3. On the exhalation, reverse the arch by slowly lifting your chin up. Look toward the ceiling and push your stomach downward to the floor. Stretch your arms straight out in front of you. On the inhalation and exhalation, repeat this happy-cat pose twice.
4. Come to sit up on your heels. Like a cat, we can change our movements and moods swiftly and gracefully.

Exercise 5.6   The Cobra (Snake) 2 min. Ages 8–12.

Goal: To stretch your back, strengthen your abdominal muscles, and focus your mind.

1. Lie facedown on a blanket, mat, or thick carpet. Place your arms alongside you, your forehead on the floor.
2. Inhale and raise your head slowly.
3. Bring your hands together under your chin. The elbows are pointing out, perpendicular to your chin.

4. Exhale, straightening your arms in front of you, lifting your head up, and arching your back. With your arms stretched in front, hold for ten seconds. Your eyes should be looking up toward your forehead and the back of your head. You can inhale and exhale in this position two more times. Let out a snakelike "hisss" on the exhale.

5. Come back into position 1, lying with your head to one side.

6. Move like a snake, hissing and wriggling across the floor, stretching and lengthening your lithe and flexible cobra-body.

Exercise 5.7   The Lion 2 min. Ages 8–12.

Goal: Strengthens upper chest, gives power to the voice, and improves self-expression.

1. Imagine yourself in the jungle, moving from being a snake in the grass to the King of the Beasts, the lion.

2. Come to a kneeling position, placing hands on tops of thighs.

3. Lift up from lower spine, bring arms overhead, as if ready to "pounce."

4. Fully open your mouth and roar like a lion, coming down to the ground in one swoop. Repeat lion's roar and pounce three times.

The lion's roar opens up the chest and throat. After roaring like a lion, you feel like you can express anything.

Exercise 5.8   Resting Pose 2–4 min. All ages.

Goal: This pose integrates all the work of the other poses, allowing for a full experience of relaxation; creates feeling of calm and well-being and of energy moving throughout the body. This pose can be done on its own if you are extremely tired or sick. Usually it is done after several poses, when you need a rest. This is a special rest because you lie down on your back and squeeze out all the space between your back and the floor.

1. Lie on your back. Breathe into the floor until your entire back is touching it and there is no space between your body and the floor.

2. Feel your tummy rising and falling with each new breath—it grows big and round when you breathe in, and becomes flat when

you breathe out. At your normal rate of breathing, breathe tension into the ground, and breathe in fresh energy.

3. Lie still like this, and feel your breath rise and fall inside your tummy. After a few minutes, slowly roll over to one side and sit up.

Variation: After lying still, imagine that you are floating on your back in a pool of perfectly clear water. The water fully supports you, so you can relax and just float.

So whatever activities you and your children prefer, moving or working the body not only can release tension but can switch our gears by shifting our brain-wave pattern from the hyperaroused beta state to the relaxed, alert alpha state (akin to "runner's high").

By helping our children keep in touch with their bodies, we can help them keep in touch with themselves. Through sports, exercise, movement, massage, and hatha yoga, they can go for the natural high of body-mind fitness.

Chapter 6

Raising a Stress-Proof Child

"I have come for my courage," announced the Lion, entering the room.

"Very well," answered the little man; "I will get it for you." He went to a cupboard and reaching up . . . took down a square green bottle . . . which he poured into a green-gold dish, beautifully carved. Placing this before the Cowardly Lion, who sniffed at it as if he did not like it, the Wizard said, "Drink."

"What is it?" asked the Lion.

"Well," answered Oz, "if it were inside of you, it would be courage. You know, of course, that courage is always inside one; so that this really cannot be called courage until you have swallowed it. Therefore I advise you to drink it as soon as possible."

The Lion hesitated no longer, but drank till the dish was empty.

—*The Wizard of Oz*, by L. Frank Baum

Just as courage already existed inside the Cowardly Lion but he didn't know it until he "drank" it, we don't always know that we can get through the trials and tribulations of our lives. We don't know if we have what it takes to meet a challenge until the situation comes up. When two people have the same difficulty, one may have what it takes to deal with it, and the second may not.

Some children, despite "strikes" against them, develop strong coping patterns, or hardiness. This is evident in observing two children in the same environment, such as siblings or

classmates, and their attitudes and adaptations to similar circumstances—for example, Ben and Jason:

Ben is nine years old and in fourth grade. Although his parents work long days at demanding jobs, they give a lot of love and attention to Ben and his younger brother, whom he adores. Ben also has serious learning disabilities. For this reason, he works extra hard in school and sees a tutor after school. Although his sessions with his tutor cut into his playtime and after-school activities, Ben doesn't mind. "I'm going to beat this thing," he says. "I know I can do it." Ben has faith in himself and in his ability to make a difference.

Jason is a classmate of Ben's. Like Ben, he has a younger brother (although Jason has little patience for his brother), hardworking and loving parents, and serious learning problems. Jason also has tutoring sessions after school but bitterly complains that "it isn't fair" that he has to miss Little League because of them. "I do everything wrong, and there's nothing I can do about it," Jason awfulizes. While Ben tries harder in school and has a positive attitude about his ability to succeed, Jason has given up on himself.

Why do some children, like Ben, seem to thrive under duress, while others, like his classmate Jason, are defeated and overwhelmed by it? The answer is what experts call "stress resistance"—an individual's ability to withstand or overcome obstacles and setbacks. A number of studies have shown that certain high-risk children, those who have grown up in economically deprived and dysfunctional families, for example, develop into happy and successful adults. Researchers have called these children "resilient," "invulnerable," and "invincible."

Stress, therefore, is not necessarily bad. What matters is how a stress is filtered through our personality, life experience, and coping skills, which together determine whether that stress will affect us detrimentally, positively, or not at all.

STRESS RESISTANCE AND TEMPERAMENT

One of our stress filters is our temperament. Drs. Stella Chess and Alexander Thomas, of the New York University Medical Center, have pioneered research on children's temperaments for more

than forty years. They have found that one of the ways babies are different from one another from the beginning of life is in their temperaments. As Chess and Thomas have written, "No single magical recipe is best for all children. What is crucial for a child's healthy development is . . . 'goodness of fit'—that is, a good match between the parents' attitudes and expectations and the individual child's temperament and other characteristics."

Goodness of fit does not create stress-free children. It simply means that a child can meet the demands of a particular situation. Some ten-year-olds, for example, may not be ready for sleepaway camp, while some eight- or nine-year-olds are. Certain schools are too high-pressured for some kids, yet not challenging enough for others. Children who master a new situation or task develop healthy coping skills and a stronger sense of their own competence, whereas those who are called on to meet demands beyond their ability may suffer from anxiety and a loss of self-esteem. There is no point in trying to shield our children from stress. Instead, we can realistically assess their capabilities and gear our expectations of them to their strengths and weaknesses as individuals.

Although temperament is one factor in how we deal with stress, obviously it is not the only factor. It may explain, however, why one child likes to throw a ball against a wall when she's feeling stressed, while another would prefer to sit and meditate. In any case, going beyond what's natural to our own particular temperament is a great way to broaden our repertory of strategies for dealing with unsettling situations.

THE THREE C'S

People with a particular group of personality traits tend to weather stress or crisis without harm to their emotional or physical health. Social psychologist Suzanne C. Ouelette of the City University of New York calls this cluster of traits "personality hardiness," and "hardy" people have these three:

Commitment: They are thoroughly involved in their activities, their family, and their community. They have strong values, and find meaning and purpose in all their pursuits.

Control: They believe they can influence events and that their own ideas and actions make a difference.

Challenge: They see change as an opportunity for growth—as a challenge, not a problem—and they are able to "roll with the punches."

In studies of people from various walks of life, Ouelette and other researchers have found that during hard times, hardy people are less likely to become ill—either mentally or physically—than other folks. These traits—commitment, control, and challenge— probably are not "built in" and can be cultivated, particularly when we're stressed. Hardiness may even develop best during times of the most stress.

Try this simple exercise of Suzanne Ouelette's to start turning your attitudes around:

Exercise 6.1   The Way You Look at It 5 min. Ages 9–12.

1. Look at a recent stressful event and think of three ways it could have gone worse.
2. Now think of three ways the experience could've gone better.
3. Looking at the ways you could have fared better, plan alternative strategies.
4. Looking at the ways it could've gone worse should provide some perspective to the situation.

Our nephew, Rami, has met a lion's share of challenges with great invincibility enhanced by a steadfast religious faith. He spent the first eighteen months of his life in an orphanage in Israel. He was then adopted by devout and loving parents, Sheila's sister and brother-in-law. The family (which grew to include his sister Sivan, adopted five years later) moved around quite a bit in Israel, and finally relocated to the Boston area. Despite adjusting to many different schools and two distinct cultures and languages, Rami's deep spiritual commitment augmented his hardy nature. This became evident during his bar mitzvah service, in a speech he made discussing a passage from Genesis. He addressed the story

of the patriarch Abraham's wanderings, in light of his own life and coming of age:

> "And God said to Abraham, leave your homeland, where you were born, your father's home, to the land that I will show you."
>
> This [passage] means a lot to me because I have moved from place to place throughout my life. I have lived in so many environments, and now I look back on my life and I try to figure out where God is trying to direct me, and what sort of life I should lead.
>
> Right now I think about it a lot because I am becoming my own boss now, and I say to myself I will take "one day at a time," meaning: I will live my life as it is and let it all fall into place later in my life. I will deal with all the difficulties and live all the [joyous occasions] to their fullest. . . . I will just have faith that everything will work out for the best, the way it has so far. . . .
>
> In that children's home I was given a lot of love and care, and I . . . am going to give charity out of my bar mitzvah money to the children's home. I hope that all other children there who are awaiting adoption also find loving and caring and devoted families such as mine.

Rami mastered the three C's of hardiness (commitment, challenge, control), as well as a fourth and fifth, caring and charity, by showing gratitude and caring to his parents and family, and by connecting (through charity) to other children with whom he shared a bond.

One way children deal with adversity, as Rami did, is by calling upon their personal values—including spiritual and religious ones. Research by Dr. Kenneth R. Pelletier of the Stanford University Medical Center supports the role of values in our health. Pelletier has interviewed prominent individuals to study the interplay among psychological factors, spiritual values, health, and success in their chosen fields. (Pelletier reported his findings

in the book *Sound Mind, Sound Body*.) "These people make decisions based on their values, which in retrospect you could say were good financial or career decisions," Pelletier says, although at the time they made those decisions they often seemed unwise. "But because they were motivated by these higher or spiritual values . . . when they acted in a manner consistent with their values, things usually worked out well. The lesson for children and for adults raising them is: Stick to your values. If you do adhere to your values, the likelihood is that you will make the right decision."

"I THINK I CAN . . ."

Most children and parents are familiar with the story "The Little Engine That Could." Through its own self-confidence—"I think I can, I think I can"—the little engine was able to pull a long and heavy train. This sense of one's ability to achieve a certain goal—what Stanford psychology professor Albert Bandura calls "perceived self-efficacy"—may be an important factor in your child's resistance to stress.

This confidence in one's ability to accomplish a difficult task may be a factor in an individual's ability to control pain. In other research, a team at the Stanford Arthritis Center led by Drs. Halsted Holman and Kate Lorig designed a health-education program for chronic arthritis patients, which consisted of six two-hour weekly sessions focusing on pain relief, medication, exercises for retaining strength and motion, patient-physician communication, and nontraditional therapies. Participants in the program had less pain and depression than patients who didn't take the course. But the researchers couldn't find any connection between the specific techniques taught in the course—such as relaxation and exercise—and the improvements in participants' health. They found, however, that the patients who had these positive changes were the ones who felt that they were able to do something about their condition and improve the quality of their lives, despite their disabling illness.

The researchers concluded that *self-efficacy* was the key fac-

tor in their success. As the participants' sense of their own competence—their self-efficacy—increased during the course, their pain decreased. Moreover, based on a follow-up study of these patients, the effects of self-efficacy seem to last over time. Four years after the six-week program, participants had significantly less pain and fewer visits to their physicians than when they entered the program, despite the fact that their disability had increased (as is usually the case with chronic arthritis).

Giving our children the message that they can master how they think and act in trying circumstances may have implications for their health as great as—or even greater than—any specific technique or exercise.

OPTIMISM

Although it is not possible, or perhaps even desirable, for us to have a positive attitude all of the time, optimists—those who generally believe that things will turn out well—appear to live longer, have better health, and catch fewer infectious diseases than do pessimists—those who have a more negative outlook on life.

In a series of scientific experiments led by Dr. Martin E. P. Seligman, a psychologist at the University of Pennsylvania, two groups of dogs received electric shocks*: The first group was able to turn off the shocks, while the second group was powerless to evade the shocks. A third group of dogs was given no shocks. The researchers then placed the dogs in another setting, in which they could easily escape the shocks by jumping over a low barrier. The dogs who previously had been able to turn off the shock jumped over the barrier, but those who had previously had no impact on the first set of shocks didn't try to escape the second set. Seligman and his coworkers concluded that these dogs had learned to be helpless. He coined the term "learned helplessness" to describe an

---

* Readers who are concerned about laboratory experiments on animals may be interested in reading Seligman's thoughtful discussion of his own struggle with this issue, in *Learned Optimism*, New York: Alfred A. Knopf, 1991, pp. 20–22.

individual's sense of having no influence over events in his or her life along with the resulting tendency to give up trying to make things better.

Whether we learn to feel helpless depends on our "explanatory style"—how we explain, or interpret, to ourselves the setbacks or triumphs in our lives. "Some people, the ones who give up easily, habitually say of their misfortunes: 'It's me, it's going to last forever, it's going to undermine everything I do,' " Seligman writes in his book *Learned Optimism*. "Others, those who resist giving in to misfortune, say: 'It was just circumstances, it's going away quickly anyway, and besides, there's much more in life.' "

Research on explanatory style suggests that, from a health standpoint, realists—those who see the occasionally harsh realities of a situation—thrive less well than optimists—those who look on the bright side of things. In our family, both our sons tend to have a "positive" explanatory style, as in "It was a hard test," or "The umpire was unfair." In the past, our tendency as parents was either to persuade them of the reality of the situation or to get them to acknowledge that the problem was at least partly their own fault. For instance, "You would've gotten a better grade if you'd have studied harder," or "You might not have struck out if you had more batting practice"—all of which might or might not be true. Although we still want our kids to take responsibility for their actions and avoid passing the buck, we now see the value of putting things in perspective (even if it's their perspective, not ours), letting go, and moving on. We can't force our kids to "learn from the experience," but we now believe they do learn, whether or not we drive the point home. Or to put it another way: too much reality is not always a good thing.

Fortunately, optimism probably can be learned (so can pessimism), and sometimes it is learned from the very challenges a child has to overcome.

LET-GO-ABILITY

When Ezra was seven or eight, he got into a horrible fight with a close friend, Scott. Both boys' faces were red with rage, their eyes

glowering at one another with intensity, as they struggled, yelling and grabbing at each other. Finally, the adults were able to separate them and talk to them reasonably. The boys sat at opposite sides of the room from each other, still breathing hard, with sweat pouring off their foreheads.

As Scott got up to walk away with his mother, he turned to Ezra and said, "Ask your parents if we can play later, OK?"

Ezra smiled at him, replied "Sure!" and then asked us, "Can Scott and I play?"

Children have an uncanny ability to let go of difficulties, anger, and "bad" feelings, which we call "let-go-ability." It's that trait that allows them to forgive their friends and bounce back after a setback, such as a poor grade or a mistake on the ball field or stage. Unfortunately, this quality is not always rewarded. In school, for example, a teacher who takes a strictly mathematical cumulative average of a child's performance throughout the term fails to fully acknowledge a child's progress. Frequently as parents, we try to get children to "hang on" to a painful experience by rehashing—undoubtedly our intention is for the children to learn their lesson—when what they want to do is chalk it up as experience and move on to the next thing.

We have learned from our children that this is frequently the healthier approach. Here's an exercise that helps a child cultivate let-go-ability. It can enable us to turn things around, by seeing that our reactions to events don't have to be based solely on emotions. We don't have to get stuck in the "quicksand" of our emotions:

Exercise 6.2   Out of Quicksand 5–7 min. Ages 8–10.
Goal: For self-control, to help solve conflicts creatively.

1. Notice when you are upset, *why* you are upset, and what it feels like. For example, "I'm so angry, he's taking my video games without permission again. I feel angry in my chest."
2. Instead of going with your usual reaction (losing your temper, getting into a fight), say the word "Quicksand." This word describes what being stuck is. If we are stuck in the feeling of anger, we cannot "climb out of it," any more than we can climb out of

quicksand. Saying "Quicksand" reminds us of that and serves as a cue to do something different.

3. Doing something different can mean becoming a witness or watcher of what's upsetting us, or telling someone how we feel: "When you do this, I feel that." It is coming from a place of power and equanimity rather than from a place of victimization or vulnerability.

4. If you are too upset to act in a detached or witness manner, take a few deep breaths or a walk. You can say "I'm rising above my [name the feeling]. I let go of it, rather than getting stuck in it." Then do what you have to do.

As we mentioned in Chapter 2, awesomizing and using affirmations are two techniques that help children feel better about themselves and let go of negative thinking. Modeling let-go-ability or helping a child to let go is another way, as in the following illustration of what a child and her mother did to transform separation anxiety.

One morning just a few weeks after starting nursery school, Samantha and her mom, Greta, arrived at school and Samantha uncharacteristically burst into tears.

"Mommy, Mommy, please don't go!" she cried.

Samantha's teacher seemed quite kind and capable as she drew her aside to talk. After a few minutes Greta hugged her daughter a final time. As she left for work, Greta thought about how, together, she and her daughter were having separation anxiety and how it would pass. The teacher would handle it.

When Greta came to pick Samantha up in the afternoon, she was surprised to find that Samantha was still sulky and upset. Again mother and teacher tried to talk to Samantha, who finally admitted she was "just having all of these bad feelings." Greta remembered something she'd tried with her daughter in the past. "You say you have bad feelings. Let's try to let go of them and do some affirmations."

Samantha immediately grew excited and said, "I have bad feelings, but I can let them go until they never come back!" She said this a few times, and feeling better, she changed it to: "When I let go of these feelings, I can talk about what's bothering me." It was as if a giant knot had unraveled inside Samantha, causing the

frown line in her forehead to unfurrow. Soon Samantha was talking and sharing her problems with her mom. On the way home, she repeated a few more times, "I let go of these bad feelings. When I let go, I can talk about what is bothering me" and added affirmations like "I am a big girl." After a while, she agreed with her mother that she didn't need to keep saying anything about the bad feelings not coming back, because they had left as she repeated, "I let go of the bad feelings."

Samantha's shift began when she acknowledged her "bad" or scary feelings. She had to let them be, before she could let them go.

A child whose self-image is underdeveloped may allow negative thoughts and words to disable her. She may believe "I am weak" or "I am stupid" or "Nobody likes me," rather than a more positive "I did a stupid thing, but I'm really smart."

Samantha's process involved many steps. The first step was acknowledging a problem, the second step was letting go of it; and the third was affirming herself in a positive way. The extent to which a child can let go allows a space, an opening for change. We can remind ourselves and our children that letting go is an ongoing activity. Simply repeating affirmations without making the effort to change or let go of negative attitudes may be like putting a small Band-Aid on a large wound—only partially helpful.

Using affirmations may also involve visualizing ourselves a certain way, breathing, relaxation, or other techniques. The smallest kid on the basketball team may do better than his bigger peers if he feels "big" about himself and sees himself succeeding. By learning to say, "I think I can," like the little engine that could, he can turn himself around.

Here is a variation on the Thought Bubbles exercise (p. 30, ex. 2.7). You can take "affirmation action" by writing an affirmation:

Exercise 6.3 Affirmation Action Untimed. Ages 9–11. (Younger children can do this with a parent.)

1. Notice when your mind is in a rut, or when you are upset.
2. Repeat this thought out loud: "I am unhappy because . . ."
3. Make two lists, one starting with "I am unhappy because . . ."

and write the reason why, such as "my teacher gives me too much homework." Start the second list with a solution statement: "I will finish all my homework and still have time to play."

Allow the two sentences to exist together, with equal weight. However, repeat only the solution statement out loud for a few minutes every night before sleep.

4. Notice after several nights if the negative or problem statement has less weight in your mind. If it does not, rewrite your solution statement and continue repeating it.

5. Notice over time any changes that you can link to your affirmation.

Dan Jansen, formerly the heartbreak kid of speed skating, having fallen and failed to win in Olympic competition, went on years later to win a gold medal. Affirmations, an important part of Jansen's preparation, may have provided him with the confidence—and edge—he lacked in the past. Jansen had been concentrating his training on the 500-meter race, but his coach was concerned that Jansen was setting himself up for a fall by putting all his eggs in one basket (especially because the 500 meters is such a short race). So, on the advice of a sports psychologist, Jansen began to focus more on the 1,000-meter race. Every night before he went to bed, Jansen did his own version of awesomizing by repeating the affirmation "I love the 1,000." The event in which he finally won the gold medal was the 1,000 meters.

THE HARDY HEART

Our coping patterns as adults—and their accompanying effects on our health—may begin in childhood, according to scientific evidence. One study found, for example, that when children were subjected to stress, those with Type A behavior—a cluster of traits including hostility, competitiveness, and impatience—had a greater tendency toward high blood pressure and higher catecholamine levels than other children.

Dr. Redford Williams, of the Duke University School of

Medicine, in his book *The Trusting Heart: Great News About Type A Behavior*, explores among other heart/health connections the relationship between hostile family environments and the health of children raised in such environments. According to Williams, criticism and punishments are two negative reinforcers that can have detrimental effects on the child's "heart," or emotionality, by teaching children to cut off or shut off their feelings, to mistrust their parents and others, and to engage in negative behaviors just to get attention, even if the attention is a punishment.

Parents can diffuse their own hostility through relaxation, meditation, religious affiliation, assertiveness (versus aggression), humor, communication (empathy versus criticism), and listening skills. In so doing, parents can become more open and trusting, and as a result their children can model more openness and trust.

Another way to help children develop healthy emotionality and a hardy heart is to build their self-esteem by celebrating their successes or praising their efforts.

For example, a teacher or parent can provide constructive encouragement rather than criticism. Dr. Ivan Barzakov, who devised a holistic educational system, OptimaLearning®, calls this approach *educative feedback*. "We allow students to succeed by suggesting they try something another way, or by praising their unique efforts," he says. "Ultimately, there is no 'right' or 'wrong' way in the learning performance; there is continuous improvement whereby the teacher or parent guides the student."

Not only should we praise and encourage our children but we should urge them to recognize their own accomplishments and those of others. Children are most likely to do so if they see their parents do so.

We tend to think of self-esteem as something we have or don't, or that someone else has more of than we do. Another way to view self-esteem is as something we and our children can build for ourselves through the activities we do. We can develop our self-esteem "muscles," just as we build our physical muscles through exercise and other physical activity. We like to think of self-esteem as a bank account, which we can add to every day. Then, when children face a "debt," a challenge such as being teased by peers or doing badly on a test, they can draw upon their

self-esteem bank account. And the interest compounds—the more self-esteem we have "saved up," the more we have to draw on to build even more. Here are some ways to build and increase self-esteem:

1. *Taking responsibility*. All children benefit from doing jobs around the house. A three-year-old can put the spoons on the table. A six-year-old can make her bed. Older children can do many chores, even making dinner one night a week.

2. *Learning the impact of our own actions and choices*. When children understand that their actions influence how people react to them and how things will go for them, they can make more proactive choices. By making choices, they can start to assume responsibility for their actions. Even making bad choices—to watch TV instead of study the extra hour—can be instructive, allowing the child to see the consequences of his actions, so that next time he can make a different choice. We can help and encourage our children to make choice statements, such as: "I will do homework for one hour and then call Jimmy," or, "It's really important to call Jimmy now, and I'll get to work later."

3. *Teaching children to set and reach reasonable goals for doing things that may be very hard or very important to them*. Help them to make lists and choice statements, such as "I want to redecorate my room. First I have to clean out all the junk in my closets and behind my bed. I will ask Mom for help. Then we will put up some new posters."

In this example, which involves cleaning chores that are difficult and may involve the child giving up some free play time, the end result—a newly decorated and tidy room—is important enough for the child that she takes part in the process from start to finish. She will be rewarded not only with a clean, new room but with an increased sense of self-efficacy.

Here's a creative exercise that helps children identify talents that may be hidden from them. Recognizing and drawing out a talent is a valuable esteem-builder.

Exercise 6.4   Personal Logo Untimed. Ages 9–12.
Goal: To help children see themselves and talents positively.

🌿 Design a logo for yourself using the initials of your name and a descriptive adjective, such as "Terrific Theresa." Add a favorite color or a picture of an activity you enjoy to your logos, such as playing basketball, painting, cooking, etc.

In one of the middle-school classes Sheila did this exercise with, ten-year-old Stephen claimed that he couldn't draw anything good about himself. "I don't have anything favorite and I can't think of any 'S' words." Teachers and classmates suggested "smart," "sensational," "sensitive," etc., but he cringed. "I'm really stupid at everything. Maybe I'm Stupid Stephen," he said. But the other students egged him on until he finally came up with "Sporty Stephen" on a motorcycle. He revealed a talent for drawing, and Sheila and his teachers used this to boost his sagging self-esteem in other lesson areas.

At another school, Theo, a soft-spoken, bright sixth grader, also suffered from low self-esteem. Like Stephen, he carved out a niche of failure for himself and almost never produced anything constructive in class. But then he won the deciding point for his "team" in a word-game contest. From that he composed a silly story using the words from the game. His writing was praised, and he wrote well in subsequent classes. In this case, "fun" was the trigger to unleashing his natural creativity, and "success" or praise counteracted his usual sense of inferiority.

One way to help students organize their thoughts is to create a visual plan educators call "mapping," "scaffolding," or "mindscaping." In her books *Maps, Mindscapes, and More* and *Mapping Inner Space: Learning and Teaching Mind Mapping,* author/illustrator and teacher-trainer Nancy Margulies describes the process she uses to help her students solve problems and to plan and execute projects. Margulies says that you start by "putting the intention down," as a central idea in the middle of a large sheet of drawing paper. Then you draw branches or lines out of the center and write down sub-ideas. She says, "You can plan out a family vacation this way. The main or central idea might be 'Disney World,' and sub-ideas might be 'What to pack,' 'Travel reservations,' 'Shopping,' etc." A mindscape like this can start during a family brainstorming session. It's creative and fun, while also teaching children to take responsibility.

"They see that they have things they have to pack or do," Margulies says.

One girl named Serika, whom Margulies worked with, drew a mindscape with the central idea being "Getting by." Serika had some problems she wished to resolve. She drew winding roads coming out of a central circle. On each line, Serika wrote a different piece of advice. The drawing process triggered her memory. She saw that in the past she had come up with solutions that had worked. These were resources she could draw upon now, too.

Mindscaping nurtures creativity while building confidence, because students see concretely that they can solve *their* problems with *their own* solutions.

Based on work Sheila has done with students, here's a mindscape you can try with your school-age child. We call it "Mindmatter," which stands for mind over matter, as well as for putting on paper the "matter" that's in your mind, so that you can do something productive with it.

Exercise 6.5   Mindmatter Untimed. Ages 7–11.

1. Make a circle in the center of a large piece of paper. Pick a topic (for instance, Homework or After-School Schedule).
2. Keep in mind that you are putting a plan on paper for solving a problem (for instance, how to get all your homework done and still have time to watch TV).
3. After you write your topic in the center, draw branches or lines out of the center. Use different-color markers for each branch. Then, using a combination of doodles and words, write everything that comes to mind on this topic (for instance, "Time schedule: 3–4 P.M. do homework," "4–4:15, practice piano").
4. When finished, take action toward meeting your goal or solving your problem.

THE BEST MEDICINE?

Still another way to build self-esteem and personality hardiness is to help children develop their sense of humor. It's been said that

laughter is the best medicine, so we can encourage our children to have fun and use good-natured humor appropriately—sometimes it's okay to be silly, sometimes it's not.

Dr. William Fry, Jr., a psychiatrist at Stanford University, found that laughter has a potent impact on our physiology: three minutes of laughter each day is equal to about ten minutes of rowing, with many of the benefits of exercise to our cardiovascular system as well as increased ventilation of the lungs. Fry also found that as laughter subsides, our blood pressure, muscle tension, and breathing and heart rates all temporarily decrease—effects similar to those found in the relaxation response.

In his now-classic book *Anatomy of an Illness*, Norman Cousins reported that when stricken with a medical condition that involved inflammation of his joints and spine so severe that it was painful for him even to turn over in bed, ten minutes of belly laughter gave him two hours of pain-free sleep.

Based on these reports it appears that laughter can be a potent de-stressor. Comic videos, joke books, tickles, and perhaps any other activity that's "fun" may be among the best stress-breakers for children.

Further research supports the notion that laughter can be a powerful antidote to harmful stress by setting in motion a cascade of beneficial mind-body interactions. Dr. Lee S. Berk, of the Loma Linda University Medical Center, and his colleagues showed a humor video with the comedian Gallagher to a group of subjects and measured several substances involved in the body's stress response, including epinephrine (adrenaline), norepinephrine (noradrenaline), cortisol (hydrocortisone), and others. The group who saw the humor video had decreased levels of epinephrine as compared with a control group. Berk calls laughter an example of eustress, or "good stress"—even though it gives us a light workout, its effects are positive.

One of the most intriguing findings of this research was this: those who were told they would see the comedy video had reduced stress hormone levels *even before they watched it!* In other words, just as our bodies can anticipate *disaster* when we expect the worst, or "awfulize," our bodies can respond to the *pleasures* we look forward to. The ramifications of this finding are amazing: children

might be de-stressing themselves simply by thinking about having fun in the near future, such as playing a game they enjoy, going on a special trip or family outing, seeing a movie or sports event, or visiting an amusement park.

Having fun can be very simple, and doesn't need to involve costly or distant expeditions. We can stock our homes with things that set the stage for fun, like board games, art materials, musical instruments, joke books (originals or store-bought), favorite video- and audiocassettes, and also blanks for taping. Some educational games, such as vocabulary- or memory-building card games (Scrabble, Concentration, chess, etc.), make our kids winners in the confidence and esteem department. Other fun activities include:

• Make up original question/answer card games, using topics of interests from the news and elsewhere.

• Hold "Saturday Night at the Old Movies" parties to watch Disney classics or funny Charlie Chaplin or Marx Brothers movies.

• Recycle old shoes and clothes to create dress-up clothes or costumes. Store in a large bin, closet, or treasure chest and use for special occasions or parties.

• Make fake cookies with play dough, or real ones, and conduct tea parties to celebrate unusual occasions, like your dog's first haircut or a snowstorm in April.

• Hold yard or tag sales to sell old books, toys, or clothes. Donate the profits to a favorite charity or neighborhood organization or project.

EMOTIONAL LITERACY

Many psychologists and educators believe that children do not learn effectively when they are emotionally blocked or troubled. Conversely, when children are allowed outlets for their emotional life and expression of feelings, they can attend to the content side of learning with much greater focus and retention. To help children become more aware of their feelings and learn to express

them more appropriately, educators have created innovative programs using a combination of social skills and stress-management training. This approach has been called "emotional literacy." It is also known as affective or social and emotional learning. Emotional literacy programs help children improve their self-esteem, manage their stress, and get along with others.

One of these programs is "Thinking, Feeling, Behaving: An Emotional Education Curriculum" for children and adolescents, developed by Dr. Ann Vernon, a psychotherapist and associate professor of counseling at the University of Northern Iowa in Cedar Falls. "Thinking, Feeling, Behaving" is based on Rational-Emotive Therapy (RET), whose premise is: What we think—that is, our beliefs—influences how we feel and act, and most important, we can learn to act and react differently than we have in the past. For example, a child who is called a name could learn to shrug it off rather than automatically getting upset and fighting with the other child. *Thinking, Feeling, Behaving* has lessons on feelings, self-acceptance, beliefs and behavior, interpersonal relationships, and problem-solving.

Learning they can react to difficult situations in new ways is empowering for children, such as the third grader who had previously been notorious for his tantrums who told Vernon, "I'm not a robot anymore. Now I'm me."

Another emotional literacy program, Social Problem-Solving (SPS) Training, teaches children coping strategies for stressful circumstances and interpersonal problems. SPS was developed by a team of Yale University psychologists and educators at the New Haven Social Development Program. They have found that SPS improves students' behavior, problem-solving ability, and relationships with their peers. SPS consists of the following steps:

1. Stop, calm down, and think before you act.
2. Say the problem and how you feel.
3. Set a positive goal.
4. Think of lots of solutions.
5. Think ahead to the consequences.
6. Go ahead and try the best plan.

Karol De Falco, a teacher in the New Haven, Connecticut, public school system, shared with us these comments from sixth graders and teachers:

"I witnessed one of my students intervene in an argument to remind his classmates about how to solve a problem. This particular student once told me the program was 'stupid' and didn't work, so I suggested he try to use it. When I later commented to him that I saw him use the steps to help his friends, he said he guessed the program was OK!"

"I had one female student who stated . . . that her favorite pastime was fighting. By the end of the lessons in problem-solving she was using the techniques and would . . . help people who were having problems in the halls with fights or quarreling."

"I believe that teaching the students the *Stop, Calm Down, & Think* before you act measure had a lot of impact on me as well. I found myself stopping in stressful situations, breathing more slowly, and trying to generate more solutions for problems I had in and out of my classroom."

"[The Social Development Project] showed me to have more responsibility, patience—a lot more— because, before, I used to have no patience. I used to scream, whatever, talk back. Now I just think, *Calm down*. . . . Later, in the future, when I grow up, I could use the techniques with my kids and stuff."

A rap song, developed by Beth Shepard of the Old Bridge, New Jersey, public school system, puts coping skills in a fun language children can understand, as follows:

Keep Calm Rap*

It's really kind of easy
A great new tool
You could use it anywhere
At home or in school

Now when you feel you're
Nervous, gonna pop;
The first step is simple
Just tell yourself to STOP!

I said STOP!
Just tell yourself to STOP!

Step 2 is just as easy
Take it down a few
With 2 deep breaths
That'll make you feel like new

Step 3 is just as simple
Two words—that's all is said
The words are "Keep Calm"
Let 'em run around your head
Keep Calm
Say it some more
And when you feel it working
You can go to Step 4
That is the last step
The step that's lots of fun
You can pat yourself upon your back
A job that's well done.

Try writing your own rap song about your favorite way or ways of coping with stress.

Actions follow thought, and thought can motivate action.

---

* Reprinted from Sixth-Grade Social Problem-Solving Module (1990–91), © 1990 Weissberg, Caplan, Bennetto, Jackson.

Sometimes we change by doing something different (instead of whining or demanding something, a five-year-old learns to ask, "May I please have?") or by thinking differently ("I'm not a baby. Only babies cry for milk. I will ask like a big girl.").

In either case, that shift from an entrenched behavior leads to hardiness, hardiness encompassing "let-go-ability" (letting go of negative attitudes, immature or inappropriate behavior) and progressive (as opposed to regressive) growth.

Sometimes children develop hardiness through reactions to circumstances of birth or upbringing, as Rami did, or in coping with illness, handicap, or chronic conditions, as we'll see and explore further in Chapter 9.

From the standpoint of temperament, some children may be more positive, optimistic, or hardy than others. We believe that these qualities are inherent in all children, but the pressures of growing up today may cloud them. We also believe we can teach children to turn around their attitude from "I won't, I can't" to "I know I can." Just deciding to do better can swing the pendulum from pessimism to optimism, and ultimately from failure to success.

The hardy child has mastered many complex social tasks, and, as a leader, can shape, build, or create healthy environments. She adjusts to less-than-ideal ones (an overcrowded classroom with a rigid teacher, for instance). She may glimpse a hopeful future while living in the present. He learns from his own trials and mistakes. The hardy child has an innate sense of self-worth and self-esteem.

In the next chapter, we'll continue to explore ways our children can feel good about themselves while moving out into the world of friendship and what we adults call "community" or "society."

Chapter 7

The Social Connection:
Helping Your Child Get Along with Others

> One day when George was skating to Martha's house, he tripped and fell. And he broke off his right front tooth. . . . The dentist replaced George's missing tooth. . . . When Martha saw George's lovely new golden tooth, she was very happy.
>
> "George! You look so handsome and distinguished with your new tooth!"
>
> And George was happy too. "That's what friends are for," he said. "They always look on the bright side and they always know how to cheer you up."
>
> "But they also tell you the truth," said Martha with a smile.
>
> —from *George and Martha*, by James Marshall

When Ezra was six, he had a sledding accident. He took a mean spin through the thick, newly fallen snow in Riverside Park into an unprotected wire fence. He was rushed to the emergency room, where he received a dozen stitches.

When he got home Ezra refused to talk to either of us, his grandparents, or his aunt and uncle about the ordeal. Shaken and upset, he could barely find a comfortable position to lie down in. But later on Ezra's best friend Jeremy came over. This was the conversation:

Jeremy: "Does it hurt?"

Ezra: "Yeah."

Jeremy: "It looks like it hurts."

Ezra: "Yeah, it really hurts a lot."

"Were you scared?" Jeremy asked.

"Kind of."

"What happened?"

"I went down the steep part and the sled just didn't stop. It slammed up against the fence. I went flying into it. My head got cut open. There was blood everywhere. My mom screamed for help, but there was no one there. So she carried me all the way up the hill. Then we got in a cab to the hospital. . . ."

"I would've been scared," Jeremy said.

"Yeah, I was."

As Ezra and Jeremy spoke, the tension in Ezra's face softened and he even smiled. His shoulders unhunched and he seemed to relax. Soon after Jeremy went home, Ezra easily fell asleep.

His friend's support ameliorated the ordeal of Ezra's sledding accident. The value of social connections—of friendship, of sharing our hurts and triumphs, of creating and building community—cannot be overestimated.

Connecting to our own self, as we've seen, helps us to connect to the self in others, bringing value and meaning to our lives. Conversely, connecting with others helps us connect with ourselves. When we don't connect with others, we risk feeling lonely and separate.

Dr. Rachel Naomi Remen has spoken eloquently about the need for people undergoing any profound crisis in their lives—such as a life-threatening illness—to connect to others. "Isolation," she says, "is the disease of our time." However, we don't need to wait for a crisis to reach out to others.

It has been suggested that social connections are life-affirming and perhaps even life-saving. Research shows that the more social ties we have, the lower our risk of dying at any given age. For example, Dr. Lisa Berkman, now at Yale University, and Dr. S. Leonard Syme, professor of epidemiology at the University of California at Berkeley, found that residents in Alameda County, California, who had more social connections—such as marriage, contact with friends and family, even membership or affiliation in a church or other group—lived longer than those with fewer social ties.

A study by Dr. David Spiegel and his colleagues at Stanford University found that women with advanced breast cancer who were receiving medical treatment and who also attended a support group lived longer than those who did not attend the support group.

Connectedness to others may be a key factor in preventing and overcoming stress. Dr. Dean Ornish, whose program for people with heart disease includes diet, exercise, meditation, stress management, and group support, has written that "in the final analysis, the perception of being isolated is a fundamental cause of why we react to the world in ways that cause us to be stressed."

Research with animals strongly suggests that social ties can buffer our response to stress. At Stanford University, for example, Dr. Seymour Levine and his colleagues subjected monkeys to stress by giving them an electric shock. Levine's group found that when a monkey who was alone received the shock, its level of cortisol, a stress hormone, rose. But if, when the monkey received the shock, it was with another monkey, its cortisol was lower than when it received the shock alone. And if paired with a monkey from a familiar group—its peer group—*its cortisol didn't rise at all in response to the shock*.

It appears that in the same way, the company of our friends, family, and acquaintances may actually reduce the effects of stress. People who have the support of friends and family, and those who belong to social and religious groups, tend to live longer and recover faster from illness than those who have weaker social-support systems, according to research studies. Feeling connected to their family, friends, community, society, and world supports children who are contending with obstacles, setbacks, and hard times.

FAMILY

As Mrs. Doubtfire, the mythical perfect nanny played by Robin Williams, said, there are many types of families: Some with one parent, some with two. Some children have stepparents, some have foster parents, some have unconventional parents.

The family, whatever its composition, is an essential social unit for the child. According to a study by family therapist Dr. Dolores Curran, certain traits are found in "healthy families," families in which family members exhibit healthy behaviors and interactions. We've included some of Curran's and added to it. Members of "healthy families":

- Spend time together
- Share responsibility
- Communicate with one another
- Hold similar beliefs
- Have a sense of right and wrong
- Respect and trust one another
- Affirm and support one another
- Respect one another's privacy
- Have a strong sense of family
- Interact in a balanced way with other family members
- Serve others

Note: Even in a "healthy family," some children are more socially skilled than others. We may say of one, "Oh, she's just a loner," or another, "He's a social butterfly." If a child seems unusually remote with his peers or can't seem to get along with any of his playmates, or if a child can't stand to play alone for a minute, we may need to help him or her to a more balanced social life. We may have to build in "playing alone" time for the overly social child, or arrange comfortable play dates for the extremely shy child.

Peer relationships are as important for the outgoing, social child who needs them to sustain his sense of self, as they are for the quiet child who finally makes a friend.

FAMILY COUNCIL

Recognizing our own social needs as well as those of our children supports all family members. In our family we've set up a council for working out problems, making decisions, and airing grievances.

During the course of the week, we save up instances of "things we want to get off our chests." By waiting until the council meets, we are less apt to "fly off the handle" and more inclined to thoughtful reflection.

We usually hold our family council on weekends, at a non-pressured time. We've also found that unless we set a specific time and day, we never get around to it. We eliminate distractions, such as TV and telephone answering, when we are meeting.

Each time a different family member leads the council. (Young children can co-moderate with a parent.) If he or she wants, the moderator proposes a particular theme, such as household chores or other family members using a person's things without permission. The moderator initiates a discussion and then takes comments, or each family member raises issues that we all then discuss. We pass a bell to whoever's speaking, which we ring at the end of our turn and pass to the next speaker. Out of the family council meetings have sprung up job charts (so that Mom doesn't get stuck cleaning up after everyone), checklists (so that we don't have to remind the kids to brush their teeth, pack their lunches, and do homework), and special privileges for the kids, such as staying up late once a week to watch a favorite TV show. We find that the family council helps us communicate with one another, find ways to help one another, and defuse potentially explosive situations.

Once, a few years ago, we found that the members of our family were being very short-tempered with each other. The kids, particularly, were yelling at one another and fighting. We immediately called a family council to deal with this situation. At the council meeting, Sheldon said, "Why don't we all give our ideas about what people in the family can do when they're feeling angry." One at a time, we went around the dinner table and gave our ideas, like this:

- Sheila: Wash dishes.
- Zachary: Have a pillow fight.
- Ezra: Tell the other person how you feel.
- Sheldon: Jump up and down.
- Sheila: Walk the dog.

- Zachary: Make funny and silly and crazy and noisy noises.
- Ezra: Listen to music.
- Sheldon: Leave the room, look in the mirror, and make funny faces at yourself.

We posted the list of ideas on the refrigerator. When family members would get angry, we'd remind each other to look at the list and follow one of the suggestions, or to come up with a new one and add it to the list.

If this is a problem in your family, you may want to try the same approach. You could start your own list, or start with ours and add your own ideas to it.

Including the whole family in taking on a problem helps support the person with the problem, and also provides the benefit of more ideas than one person could come up with on her own.

Try this approach when someone in the family is "nervous"—for example, when one of the parents or kids has to make a lengthy presentation at school or work, a big test, or a performance. Hold a family council and ask everyone in the family to come up with ideas of Things You Can Do When You're Nervous. Or focus on an area that continues to hassle family members. On weekends, we found that Zach took glee in waking up his brother. We asked him to help solve this problem he had of waking a sleepy and mad brother up. He came up with:

What to do when people are sleeping

- Get dressed
- Cuddle
- Color or read
- Play games
- Draw
- Dream
- Meditate
- Have your own breakfast

Sometimes families can meet to do something fun or to tackle a chore or project together, such as finally putting all the

loose photos in albums. Friends and neighbors can be included in the spirit of fun.

Here are two such enriching activities:

Exercise 7.1   Family Treasure Chest Untimed. All family members (all ages).
Goal: To develop self-esteem, respect for belongings, generosity. To sharpen communication skills. To have fun.

1. Pick a leader. Leader gives directions and times a Treasure Hunt (5 to 15 minutes). Each player looks through the house and selects five or six personal "treasures," objects with special meaning. These could be baseball cards, an Indian feather, a crystal, a shell or rock, a handmade art or craft object, a doll, a book, or a toy.
2. When time is up, all players gather in front of a chest (a large decorated carton will do). Optional: Older children may write a descriptive list ("birthday card from Aunt Shirley"); younger children may draw pictures of objects, or dictate a list.
3. Objects are then ceremoniously placed in the chest for later play. Parent or leader can talk about respecting one another's things, and that caring for treasures is like caring for ourselves.

Exercise 7.2   Family Wall Untimed. Children ages 6–12 and their parents.
Goal: To foster creative expression, connectedness, self-concept. To see self as part of a larger picture. This is fun to do on a weekend or rainy day.

1. Tape a large roll of mural paper to a wall in the hallway, basement, or any room. May do alone or with family.
2. Select photos, magazine cutouts, and other collage materials that symbolize yourself and your family. Pick a theme, such as "family vacations," or place pictures chronologically.
3. Design and lay out the mural. Use glue stick or tape to put on the cutouts. Draw in background with felt-tip markers, crayons, and pencil. Add any captions or dates that you like.
4. Periodically add significant pictures or photos. Mark special

events or milestones, such as births, birthdays, first tooth, school play, getting a new pet.

COOPERATIVE LEARNING

For many children, friendship is the most important aspect of school. Because children's peer relationships can often be competitive, cruel, and rejecting, it is important for parents and teachers to encourage and model cooperative, thoughtful, and considerate behavior toward others.

Cooperative learning, a current trend in education, fosters group cooperation, participation, and communication with the aim of developing a sense of community and an appreciation of diversity.

For example, in third-grade teacher Ann Meyers's classroom in Manhattan Beach, California, children learn to appreciate one another or to express their displeasure in a constructive way. In a "friendship circle," the class passes around a velvet heart, and whoever is holding the heart can speak. A student may say, for instance, "Thank you, Sharon, for helping me spell words I didn't know." (Meyers encourages the kids to appreciate classmates other than their best friends. The children also have the option to pass.) Other times they may express a grievance, so long as they do it in a respectful way, following the form "I do not like it when you . . . I prefer when you . . ." For instance, "Randy, I do not like it when you take my pencil without asking. I *prefer* you ask me first."

In cooperative classrooms such as Meyers's, students learn about community of different cultures—and about caring through social action programs, like collecting money for and serving meals to the homeless.

RITUAL: CONNECTIONS IN TIME AND SPACE

One of the reasons the cooperative-learning programs are so powerful is that they incorporate ritual. Ritual connects us to our spiritual side, to our values, and to others. The original meaning of

the word "ritual" is to fit or join. Rituals, then, are acts of connection, activities that join us together or that join us to a tradition, community, or purpose, or to the divine. In its highest form, a ritual is a routine act made special or sacred. In a moment, the ritual act links thought and deed. We align our body, mind, spirit, voice, and vision.

Most families have their own rituals for celebrating special occasions, such as holidays, birthdays, graduations, and anniversaries. But, often without even realizing it, we weave ritual through our daily lives. Children have bedtime rituals, including perhaps a bath, changing into pajamas, a story, a prayer, a cuddle. We can also celebrate small victories in a special way—a good report card, athletic achievement, scout's merit badge, or performance in a school play or concert can be met with "We're Proud of You" signs, balloons, cards, little gifts, treats, or flowers.

Not all rituals are spiritually based. Rituals such as school dismissal procedures or afternoon snack are fairly mundane. The regularity of these rituals reassures children and helps to order an often chaotic universe. Ritual can restore frayed nerves, worn bodies, indeed the very seams of the family fabric. Many families rise above the daily grind by praying or saying grace at the dinner table.

In our home, we celebrate the Jewish Sabbath on Friday night. We light the candles and bless the children, and then we all recite prayers over the challah bread and wine (grape juice). A family we know in Northridge, California, enacts a Friday-night thank-you ritual with their four sons. The children thank both of their parents for whatever they have done for them in the course of the previous week. We were impressed by this ritual of gratitude and decided to adopt it and to take it a step further, so that we all thank each other. The children thank us and one another, and then *we* thank the kids and each other. In so doing we appreciate one another, acknowledge the unique contribution of each family member, and learn not to take one another for granted. Thanks can be for something special, such as "Thanks, Dad, for taking us sledding. It was really fun." Or: "Thanks, Mom, for making me go to the museum. I didn't think I would like it, but I did." Or it can be for something routine, such as "Thanks, Dad, for making my lunch." Or: "Thanks, Mom, for

picking me up at school and taking me to soccer practice." We thank the kids for specific ways they help around the house ("Thanks for giving the dog a bath"), their initiative ("Thanks for practicing your typing without waiting for me to remind you"), their ideas ("Thanks for suggesting we all go boating"), or just for sharing their time or talents with us. Even during difficult or exasperating times, we thank each other "for just being you."

The family council we described above was inspired by rituals such as Council, which is part of the Mysteries program, originally developed at the Crossroads School in Santa Monica, California. The Council process has been introduced to educators and schools through the writings and trainings of Jack Zimmerman, president of the Ojai Foundation, and originator of the Mysteries program. This curriculum and methodology is now being disseminated throughout North America under the leadership of Shelley Kessler, former chair of the Crossroad's Human Development Department and now a consultant in emotional and social learning.

In a Goals Statement, the Mysteries faculty wrote, "Self-destructive behavior now prevalent among our nation's youth has been attributed to low self-esteem, social isolation, stress and poor decision-making skills. Mysteries seeks to prevent such behavior by providing students with information and decision-making skills, but even more important, by giving young people a sense of their own lovability, competence, power, identity, self-esteem, joy and communion with others."

During Council, which is derived from ceremonies of indigenous cultures worldwide, students pass an object such as a "listening" stone, stick, or wand around the circle and speak in turn. We chose a bell for our meetings, and we know of teachers who use the rubber spindly Koosh balls.

Council fosters "deep listening," Kessler says, which means "listening between the lines—that is, hearing people's feelings and intentions as well as their words. Deep listening breaks the habit of *reactiveness*—that is, the tendency to interrupt with reactions such as defensiveness, judgment, and hostility before one has taken the time to listen to and process completely what the speaker is saying."

"The miracle of Council," Kessler adds, "is that quiet and shy members of the group or family begin to speak, surprising everyone with their wisdom. Active members gain the capacity for listening and appreciation for what others have to say."

Kessler shared with us an example of how rituals such as Council have the power to transform and uplift everyday concerns:

> I sit in a circle with my seventh-grade class. Thirteen wiggly twelve-year-olds sit on the floor preparing for council. I ask if someone would like to dedicate the council. Tradition has it that there are one or two dedications. But today, the dedications just keep coming. "I want to dedicate it to my new cat." "I want to dedicate it to my grandfather who is in the hospital." "I want to dedicate it to my aunt who just died." "I want to dedicate it to my new baby brother—we just finished the adoption stuff and now he's really ours."
>
> As I watch and listen as these "dedications" keep coming, I begin to see a pattern. What do they choose to bring to their dedications? They are using this occasion, this secular form, to honor, bless, or "pray" for those in their lives who are in the midst of the great transitions, or passages of life—birth, death, grave illness. How do they know to do this? I watch and wonder and breathe a deep sigh of appreciation that these little people have the instincts to bring such care and love and healing to create a sacred moment in this classroom.

Create ritual or sacred time, as formal or informal as you like. Rituals can help children learn to give through watching their elders and in doing activities together, such as:

1. Working on a family photo album or scrapbook together, assigning different tasks, such as photographer, photo organizer or editor, labeler and designer of photos on the page. It's rewarding to recollect a special occasion, such as a family trip, confirmation, graduation, birthday, or a relative's engagement or wedding.

For example, for Ezra's bar mitzvah, we took photos taken across his life span, color-xeroxed, laminated, and then captioned them, and used them as decorative table settings.

2. Inviting guests for a special or holiday dinner, for a family council, or for engaging in a regular musical or sport activity or social action project, are some examples.

3. Asking each member or guest to bring a "family heirloom" recipe to a special dinner, and then tell about the person who originated the recipe.

HELPER'S HIGH

Acts of service not only fill a social need but also help the children involved in these activities by sensitizing them to the needs of others, translating positive values into action, and giving them the powerful experience that their actions do make a difference. Service is a tangible way for children to connect with their community and society at large.

As children and their parents volunteer even in small ways—fixing up a community center or playground; helping at or donating items to a homeless shelter; tutoring children with learning deficits or disabilities—they can enhance their own health and reduce their anxiety about all the problems in the world. In a survey of volunteers led by Allan Luks, executive director of Big Brothers, Big Sisters, New York, and author of *The Healing Power of Doing Good*, volunteers reported that helping others brought them a sense of personal well-being, or "helper's high." And a conference of scientists and health practitioners on the health benefits of helping reported that one benefit of helping others—the belief that one can make a difference—"contributes to a longer and healthier human life."

The report hypothesized that altruistic behavior can reduce feelings of helplessness and depression and hence enhance health. In his classic *The Stress of Life*, Hans Selye coined the phrase "altruistic egoism," or selfish altruism. That feeling of warmth from doing good may well come from endorphins—the brain's

natural opiates—which have also been linked to the highs we feel from running and meditation. Involving children in altruistic behaviors can enrich their own lives while benefiting others.

FEELING CONNECTED

A great way to foster connections and cooperation is through group activities such as bike riding, camping, or hiking. Here are two exercises for getting in touch with others:

Exercise 7.3   Starfish 5–8 min. Ages 7–10.
Goal: To help children connect with others through exercise. To learn to read cues and "follow the leader" in a fun way; as a pleasant stretch to energize and de-fatigue the body. To build group synergy and cooperation.

1. Create a circle with at least three people. This is great to do with a group of friends, all family members, or in a class.
2. Sit in a circle with your legs in a wide V, and the soles of your feet touching the soles of the people next to you. Rest your hands on your knees.
3. Designate one person the leader. The leader stretches over either the right leg, left leg, or center of the body. Everyone else follows.
4. You may go in turns (consecutively or any way) so that each circle member gets to lead. Play music if you like.

Exercise 7.4   "Cellular" Breathing 3–4 min. Ages 7–12.
Goal: To develop empathy and a sense of kinship, and to send positive energy to another person.

1. Sit back-to-back on two chairs or stools.
2. With eyes closed, breathe in and out. Feel the other person's back against yours.
3. Imagine that you can feel the cells of the other person's back against your back, as you both breathe in and out for a few minutes.

4. What does it feel like? See if you can pick up any information about the other person.
5. Tell each other what you learned about one another.

Locating oneself on the continuum of community is a valuable support for children. Starting with their family of upbringing, children become socialized by having to share with and care for others in their family, whether a sibling, a pet, or someone else's feelings. In this way, children can cross the bounds of an egocentric existence ("the world revolves around me") and become more giving to others.

Obviously, we live in a world filled with other people. The extent to which we live full lives depends, in large measure, on making connections with others—through acts of kindness, ritual, community, and other social activities.

We can also connect with something larger than ourselves by taking a hero's journey—transforming our understanding through looking at mythic and real heroes—and exploring our common human heritage in an uplifting way.

Chapter 8

Taking a Hero's Journey

"Listen to me, children of the Bright Country, and hear the great deeds of ages past. . . . Centuries of law and learning reside with our minds. Thus we serve the kings with the wisdom of history, bringing to life the lessons of the past so that the future may flourish.

"Listen, then, to the story of Sundiata, the Lion King, who overcame all things to walk in greatness."
—from *Sundiata, Lion King of Mali*, by David Wisniewski

Thus begins the story of Sundiata, a prince of Mali during the time of expansion and conquest in Africa, some 800 years ago. Sundiata, who as a small child could neither walk nor speak, was scorned and banished by his stepmother. In exile, Sundiata overcame great obstacles. He fought an evil sorcerer. Despite his afflictions, Sundiata developed many powers that enabled him to conquer his enemies. After his final victory, he addresses his nation with compassion and vision:

"Hatred drove me from this land because of what I seemed to be: a crawling child, unworthy of respect and unfit to rule. . . . Now I return as your king. Henceforth, none shall interfere with another's destiny. You, your children, and your children's children shall find their appointed place within this land forever."

This came to pass and Sundiata, the Lion King, ruled the Bright Country for many golden years.

Though Sundiata's boyhood was shattered, he heeded destiny's call, and came to save his land and rebuild it from ruin. From the moment he left home, he began a heroic journey that ultimately led to his personal transformation and the saving of his people.

Seeing how others seize and make real their ideals, goals, or life's mission can help us learn how we can do the same for ourselves and our children. We call this taking a hero's journey.

The journey through childhood is a journey toward development—mental, physical, social, and spiritual. Just as we would want to protect our children from environmental factors, such as air or water pollution, that might harm them, we may also wish to shield them from questionable heroes and role models we fear will pollute their minds. Many parents are concerned, for example, about the violence shown on popular cartoons, including "Teenage Mutant Ninja Turtles" and "Mighty Morphin Power Rangers." And as our children get older, we are alarmed at the often violent, obscene, racist, and sexist lyrics of the latest skinhead rock stars and gangster rappers.

These images are all around, and it may feel like a losing battle trying to combat their influence on our children. It's helpful to gain some perspective on our children's choice of heroes. The warrior is the overriding archetype in our society. The notion that we can overcome any difficulty, slay the proverbial dragon and defeat the forces of evil, is not only personified in children's comic books, cartoons, and toys—it is woven into the fabric of American myth. Children love the vivid and distinct images of brightly colored heroes with rippling muscles. On a deeper level, they are drawn to the simple black-and-white tug-of-war between good and evil and may feel reassured when the forces of good triumph. Parents may feel more comfortable with Care Bears and Smurfs, but to older children these characters are considered uncool compared with Power Rangers, Ninja Turtles, and X-men.

The question of whether to let children watch these characters on TV and read their comic books is controversial, and parents should set the limits they feel comfortable with. We find it somewhat unrealistic to ban these shows and comics (although we have banned televised wrestling matches in our home), given

their pervasiveness. However, we think it's important for parents to discuss our concerns about these heroes with our kids and to balance these images with those of other types of heroes, real and imaginary—such as people who perform service to our community or who are nice to everyone. We may also need to work hard to become the kind of role models we would like to be, by curbing our own violent and aggressive behaviors.

According to Dr. Lois Holzman, a developmental psychologist and a professor at Empire State College in New York City, learning that contributes to children's development occurs when children are supported to "stretch"—to go beyond themselves. Babies "creatively imitate" the speech gestures and actions of their caregivers. So, too, children—and adults—need to go beyond themselves. At the Barbara Taylor School in Brooklyn—Holzman is also the school's director—the teachers are explicit in their encouragement of children creatively imitating one another's strengths. For instance, a six-year-old might learn responsibility from an eleven-year-old by working with her to clean the kitchen after lunch. A twelve-year-old looked directly at an eight-year-old having a temper tantrum and said, "Imitate me when I'm angry instead of being you now."

Holzman says that children's negative or asocial behaviors lessen when together they take responsibility for teaching one another new ways to be. When children are encouraged to creatively imitate others—to *perform*—they are creating new options of how to behave and feel in situations. The teachers direct the learning situations without assuming authoritarian roles, and when students teach one another, they in turn "creatively imitate" their teachers' nonauthoritarian approach. The Barbara Taylor School's use of play and creative imitation is based on the developmental theories of renowned Russian psychologist Lev Vygotsky. The goal is for students to learn in a way that contributes to their intellectual, social, emotional, and cultural development.

Similarly, in our homes, we can learn to creatively imitate the strong points of other family members. In our family, for example, Sheila is well organized, Ezra is decisive, Zach is creative, and Sheldon is a good mediator. So if we need to make a

difficult decision, we ask Ezra how *he* would do it, and/or we "perform" Ezra's decisiveness—that is, we imitate it. Or if we need to come up with a creative solution to a problem, we might ask Zach, and then *perform* Zach's creative approach, instead of doing it our own way.

Because we learn virtually everything we know by imitating role models, we strongly advocate encouraging children to have mentors, such as an adult friend, an admired teacher, or an older relative. (Our children, for example, have an "honorary grandmother," Mary, who always shows up to give them support at concerts and graduations.)

JOURNEYS INWARD

One way children affirm who they are is by sharing in family or group rituals. Taking a hero's journey signifies more than visiting a family or national landmark. Heroes' journeys lead us inward to the landscape of common dreams, and to the birthplace of myth. They are metaphors for growth and they help us to change.

Heroes' journeys may start with finding role models and learning what they have done to achieve their goals. Because heroes are larger than life, their actions are not limited to any particular event. Identifying with the limitlessness of the heroes' powers allows children to reach beyond themselves and touch the highest. (By the highest we mean their full potential, whereas in myth symbols of the highest include infinity or heaven.)

As Carol S. Pearson writes in her book *The Hero Within: Six Archetypes We Live By*, "Heroes take journeys, confront dragons, and discover the treasure of their true selves. Although they may feel very alone during the quest, at its end their reward is a sense of community; with themselves, with other people, and with the earth."

In his many books on myth, Joseph Campbell explores various types of heroes, and from him we can surmise the value of introducing our children to mythic and transformative heroes. First, in myth and in history, is the warrior hero, who is by nature the "champion not of things become (fact) but of things becom-

ing (creative life)." This hero's enemy, be he a monster or tyrant, is "the champion of prodigious fact," one who can slay dragons and perform terrible feats. As we see throughout the story of Sundiata, the "fact" of the enemy's existence is eventually defeated by the warrior hero, who is in harmony with the powers and properties of "divine right" or the living God. The hero's deed is "a continuous shattering of the crystallizations of the moment."

The Old and New Testaments abound with stories of heroes who conquer overwhelming foes, such as Abraham, who rejected his father's pagan worship of idols, and set off to find the One God; or David, the lad who slew the giant Goliath with his slingshot. Joseph, one of Jacob's twelve sons, was scapegoated by his brothers, sold into slavery, ending up shackled in Egypt. However, Joseph's gift for prophecy allowed him to advise the Egyptian pharaoh. He rose up from his humiliation (at the hands of his brothers) and became a great seer and leader, a redeemer or savior hero. Perhaps his greatest feat of heroism was forgiveness, forgiving and therefore saving his father and brothers. He helped (rather than spurned) them in their time of distress and famine. Savior heroes often aid and so uplift their enemies.

Ancient religious traditions are peopled with heroes who are both godly (such as the Indian Krishna and Rama) and those who are anointed to divine roles but prone to human flaws (such as Moses, King David, and the apostles). Sharing stories of these heroes with our children is inspiring. In the short run, we may want to begin with popular heroes, such as the sword-wielding, swashbuckling heroes of media, the archetypal do-gooders. From these familiar heroes we can go on to what Campbell calls a higher order of heroes, those whose primary purpose is not simply vanquishing the enemy but to redeem or save their people. The savior heroes save their people both physically and spiritually. They are considered to be divine or almost divine incarnations capable of demonstrating larger-than-life powers, such as seeing into the future or altering the course of destiny by certain actions. Such heroes are found worldwide, in cultures from Africa to Japan to Oceania, and is typified by (native American) Jicarilla Apache, Killer-of-Enemies, who proclaims, "The world is as big as my body. The world is as large as my world. And the world is as large as my

prayers. . . ." These types of heroes draw upon "supernatural powers" and "magic" in a way that resonates with the current use of affirmation, visualization, alternative healing techniques, or spiritual disciplines.

The saint heroes go beyond even the redeemers. Once they complete their tasks of redemption, they live out their earthly days not in performing tasks or teaching, but in becoming one with the Supreme Principle. Their earthly missions are complete and they are halfway to heaven.

REAL-LIFE HEROES

Parents can help by sharing tales that have been passed down from one generation to the next. Children often identify easily with family heroes—for instance, the ancestor who first came to this country. Many of these ancestors endured hardships, such as poor immigrants who dreamed the streets of America were paved with gold and wanted a better life for themselves and their children, or ancestors brought over as slaves.

We can also identify with heroes who have attained a significant achievement, whether overcoming prejudice, illness, or overwhelming odds to succeed—people such as Helen Keller or Martin Luther King, Jr.

Today, many kids revere "heroes" their parents may find it hard to appreciate, such as sports legends and other celebrities. Often, the child is identifying with the achievement—the ability to dunk a basket or play guitar—rather than the moral fiber of the individual. (Although some sports and entertainment figures have certainly exemplified heroic qualities—Arthur Ashe, for example.) In our culture we are attracted to commercial success, wealth, and fame. But hero worship can also exalt the fulfillment of potential in any arena. It is not surprising that posters of basketball superstar Michael Jordan, who seems to defy gravity as he soars through the air, are commonly found on the bedroom walls of young fans. But many are also impressed by Jordan's closeness to his family.

We believe it is important to expose our children to individ-

uals who reflect heroic qualities we value, a sentiment expressed by Geoffrey Canada, chief executive officer of Rheedlen Center for Children and Families, a group that aids poor children. "I desperately want to be a children's hero. . . . You see, children here in New York City need heroes because a hero summons up images of supernatural powers. Heroes were meant to slay dragons and monsters, and far too many of our children face monsters every day."

In the same vein, Linda Lantieri, national director for the National Center for Resolving Conflicts Creatively—a school-based nonviolence program—says that students need to "see that the real heroes and sheroes are not the Rambos of the world but those people who are willing to search for nonviolent solutions to difficult and complex problems."

CREATING OUR OWN MYTHIC HEROES

Children can look within and explore the lush gardens of their imaginations. There they can meet heroes of courage and faith, heroes they either create or who arise full-blown from, as Carl Jung calls it, the "collective unconscious," or from—as viewed by ancient religious cultures— "heavenly realms."

Children can also physicalize the feeling of hero by doing hatha yoga postures that are fun and enlivening. They are called hero or warrior (which is a type of hero) poses:

Exercise 8.1 Hero Pose
1 min. Ages 6–12.
Goal: To stretch torso and legs. To expand and open the whole body. To help prepare us mentally to face the challenges of daily life.

Sitting like a hero prepares you to stand like a warrior.

1. Sit on your heels. Keep your knees together.
2. Lower buttocks to floor, keeping the feet alongside the hips with toes pointing backward. The tops of the feet should be resting on the floor. If this is uncomfortable, place a small rolled blanket or towel under the knees and under the tops of the feet.
3. Inhale, raising arms in an overhead stretch. Press the palms toward the ceiling. Exhale and lower the arms. Repeat two or three times for one minute.

Exercise 8.2   Warrior Pose 2 min. Ages 6–12.
Goal: To center energy and strengthen muscles. To make us aware of our inner and outer strength.

Starting the day as a spiritual warrior, one who fights inner battles as well as outer battles (such as the battle to think well about yourself) and hassles, begins with this steadying and strengthening pose.

1. Stand straight and tall. Bring your legs several feet apart, turning the front left foot so it points straight out in front of you, and the back right foot at a sixty-degree angle, or pointing to the side wall.
2. Inhale, raise arms overhead, and place palms facing each other about two inches apart.
3. Exhale, lowering the chest slightly to face the left leg.
4. Inhale and straighten up from the base of the spine.
5. Exhale, bending the left knee and thigh until they are parallel to the floor.
6. Hold steady for a count of twenty-five or thirty, while breathing into the abdomen. Gently let go of any tension in back or shoulders, while mentally repeating, "I am a warrior, ready to face my day bravely and with strength." You can also make up your own warrior phrase.
7. Repeat this pose on the other side. Then do this exercise again.

Exercise 8.3 Warrior in Motion (Variation on 8.2)

Instead of chest facing forward, you'll be moving from the frontward position of the basic warrior pose to the side, extending the arms out to form a T, each hand pointing to opposite walls, like this:

1. Plant the right foot firmly on the floor several feet in front of the left foot. Heel of the right foot should be in line with the arch of the left foot.

2. Inhale, bringing arms to shoulder level and out, so that the right hand is pointing to the front wall and the left hand to the back wall.

3. Exhale, so that the right knee and thigh are parallel to the floor and knee is just above heel.

4. Stretch into the back of left leg by digging heel into the ground. Head is in alignment with base of spine. Turn head to look to either side, then bring it back to center. Hold, maintaining the steadfastness of the warrior.

5. Repeat for thirty seconds a warrior phrase, such as "I am ready to face the day with the strength and vigor of a warrior."

Draw a picture of yourself as a warrior, or write your own warrior phrase.

If we were to create perfect heroes for today's youth, they might resemble their mythic predecessors, but with missions far more global and less confined to one culture. We call these "new" heroes planetary heroes. They could help solve earthly disasters such as the destruction of the ozone layer, and could wage battle against poverty, crime, pollution, and racism in the larger war against an ignorant humanity.

Planetary heroes could help prevent us—the human race, that is—from repeating mistakes we can no longer afford to make, as Campbell says, by "illuminating hints to an inspired past."

Our children can create, draw, or visualize these heroes. At home, we can direct hero-making and play activities. We can encourage letter writing to or tape recording of older relatives, whose journeys such as crossing oceans or overcoming ethnic or racial barriers inspire our youngsters.

We have asked a lot of children about their heroes. Sheila, especially, visited classrooms and led activities based on creating heroes. Here's what happened with a group of Manhattan second graders during several visits to their classroom:

The room was richly decorated with artwork, pillows, and rugs in one corner, worktables in another. Children seemed to pile up on each other during independent work time. Several of the boys had trouble working on their own, and were wiggling in and out of various Transformer (as in toy) positions while poking their neighbors.

Sheila decided to channel the students' energy into the hero project. She asked them to imagine themselves as heroes saving the planet. "You can be a giant gobbling-up-the-garbage machine, or a swirling clean-up-water-pollution machine." Suddenly the fidgeters perked up. They got up and moved around the room as heroic, powerful machines. Soon most of the others joined them.

Some of the children, particularly a group of girls, had trouble coming up with heroes or models other than rather flat TV characters, some of whom were no more than "commercials" for dolls and toys. Sheila suggested that they think in terms of models or heroes that had qualities they'd like to possess, like being extra smart, kind, strong, or helpful. They could also think of themselves as possessing these qualities. She then led them in a guided imagery exercise to visualize these heroes and models and their special qualities. Eventually, models, heroes, and heroines combining the brave "male" warrior characteristics and the nurturing "female" characteristics came out of the imagery work. Jennifer, for instance, drew "Judy the Magic Bear," who at first glance appears docile but performs magnificent feats, such as flying through the air and vacuuming up air pollution.

Tavor's wonderful Robot Hand Woman (written in another class) also combined feminine and masculine characteristics in an original and magical way:

What Robot Hand Woman Does

Robot Hand Woman has big hands for a reason. She can clean up a room in one second! She can do your

homework in two minutes! She cleans up the whole state of Manhattan in a day! And she throws robbers and bad men or women in jail. If she puts her hands around you she has special powers and her powers will heal any bad germ in your body in five minutes. She has a squirt gun in her nose for April Fool's Day and . . . when there is a fire her window eyes open and water squirts out and puts out the fire. Whoever claps the loudest wins a prize. She always wins because of her big hands. That's why she has so many medals.

The End.

(Tavor, age 9)

Students in another school also drew heroes. Sheila asked them to use themselves as springboards, starting with letters from their names or drawing themselves doing something powerful. Some of the students drew with vivid sureness as if the image already existed within them and just needed to be put on paper. Others needed more coaxing. Sheila asked these students to come up with qualities they liked about themselves. Then she led all the students in guided imagery, after which they all came up with drawings of models they aspire to, including basketball stars in dazzling jump shots and rock singers in stunning costumes. Then the students stood up in front of the class, and showed and explained their drawings in relation to themselves. The students generally started off shy and embarrassed, but as they discussed extraordinary heroic qualities, they grew enthused. It was as if they had just discovered that they had heroic potential that could manifest.

Here is one drawing exercise that helps children describe their hero potential, enabling it to bloom:

Exercise 8.4   Wish Picture 10 min. Ages 4–8.

Goal: To develop self-concept and highest potential. To see oneself as manifesting one's wishes or life's purpose.

1. Divide a large sheet of paper in half. On the left side draw a portrait of how you look now.

2. On the right side draw a "wish" portrait, how you'd like to be. It can be goal oriented, such as "I want to dance more gracefully" or "I want to run faster," or fulfill a future vision, such as "I want to be an astronaut [or ballerina, or fireman]."

3. Write a caption under each, such as "The Real Me at Age 7" and "Who I'd Like to Be." Display or hang up your portraits any way you like. You may greet them silently or aloud several times a day.

You may also write several sentences on how you will become who you'd like to be.

Developing heroic qualities can happen in the community and school as well as at home. In schools across the country children are making the hero connection, feeling good about themselves and others.

The Margaret Allen Elementary School in Nashville, Tennessee, established a Super Kids project, in which "regular" and "disabled" students worked together to produce and perform a play about superheroes for the community. The play was a vehicle for teaching about friendship and helping. For instance, the students with speech or hearing disabilities taught the others to communicate with signs and gestures. A mother of one of the disabled students wrote that "the children sang about being super heroes who wear super capes and fly across the sky—they do 'superdeeds' and help out the universe and always save the day."

During the regular school year, special-education teacher Donna Steer Friedman said that the resource room children (who have mild learning disabilities) help out the severely disabled students, usually at lunch, gym, or recess. According to Friedman, who helped pilot the program, this greatly increases their sense of self-esteem. Instead of seeing themselves as needing help, students who attend the resource room see themselves as valued helpers.

Other students (so-called nondisabled) visited the students with disabilities during their regular classes, acting as their tutors. By matching mentally challenged students with those in the general student body, all students learned that they have no boundaries and that they are more than their labels.

Friedman is now taking the Super Kids concept into other classrooms in Knoxville, strengthening the level of commitment to performance. Creating theater presents challenges to all the children, with the opportunity for all of them to grow and shine.

Children can take the hero's journey in a combination of settings, whether in a highly structured stage performance or an art class. Working with their imagination and the arts allows them to try out roles they ordinarily wouldn't. A shy child who stars in a play may become less shy. An inarticulate child may become expressive in the vivid pictures she draws.

When children make the stuff of fancy real, when they bridge their inner and outer worlds and take on the heroic qualities of models and superheroes, they empower themselves. They learn that they can be leaders, creators, and shapers—that they can change their world.

To begin a program of hero exercises at home, do any of the hatha yoga poses in this chapter. Choose any of the meditation, relaxation, visualization, or other exercises in the book that help you step out of your usual role.

You and your children may also wish to seek out and visit friends, relatives, and members of your community whom you see as leading lives of hidden or not-so-hidden heroics—for instance, a neighbor who is an advocate for the handicapped or who delivers meals to homebound sick or elderly people.

Finally, encourage your child to create an art project or a story about a hero. You can make one, too. Here is one boy's planetary heroes story:

Captain Planet and the Swamp Thing

by Ilan (age 7)

One day there were two Superheroes. They were doing nothing and they had a secret mission to save the earth from the evil Unmen. Evil Unmen are trying to pollute the world by spreading toxic wastes over the earth. The alarm to save the world went off. Then they said, "We have to save the earth."

They got in their boogey board and they were off.

When they got there they fought with the Unmen. The Unmen tried to throw toxic waste at them. Soon the Unmen were finished. They said "Hey, dude! We finished off some more of them."

The End.

(P.S. The Unmen lost).

A group of third graders in New York City created heroes who could help kids or who make the world a better place.

Heroes who help kids:

(Quadruplets) They separate and Maggie tells you everything in school. Lola with a snap of her finger gives you money. Lili tells your future. Anna has all the powers in the world.

Mr. Homework if you scream homework he will come thru your window and say I will do your homework—any subject! and then you get all your answers right because he is very very smart. He always brings candy so you can eat when he does your homework.

Heroes who help us change the world:

Palee alloyed liquid metal crime fighter can transform into almost anything that he touches except for complex machines.

The *nothing man* can do anything but mostly clean the planet and make it a better place to live and be on.

Power diamond can do anything and can turn anybody into a diamond. She can tell the future and hear a lot of things.

Dot man can do anything to help people on the planet by pressing one of the buttons on him.

Ms. Eye Seeing Hero can see miles away and if anything is wrong she helps by talking to the people one at a time so it stops them from fighting. She is also *Big Face* and she can give people rides to work.

Susan Stretch can see and smell anything 35 miles away (and

closer). She can stretch her arms and legs 11 miles away (or closer). She can fly with her hair. Her stretching power can save and help people in trouble. She can run 18 miles an hour.

The Problem Stopper uses rocket boosters, a peacegun, a curegun, a land equality gun, a cleaning gun, and a crime stopping gun.

Educator Problem Stopper educates people for anything with a brain gun and book gun . . . does all your reading homework. The 4,000-year-old man does your social studies homework. The blabbermouth does your language homework. Math man does your math homework.

SuperBird flies around the world and rescues people he also saves people when they're about to crash.

Mrs. Eyeball watches people and helps if they're doing something bad.

Cheerio saves poor people.

Mega Curer has saved 8189 people from cancer and 5022 people from AIDS. He did amazing things for drug attacks [addicts] and that's how he became Mega Curer.

Super Spaceman puts drugs and diseases and weapons into spaceships and launches them into space.

Big Fingers can take people anywhere so they won't use cars and pollute the world.

Peace Person lives in a natural volcano. When the mayor needs him, the volcano erupts and peace person comes out.

Chapter 9

Special Situations

"It's going to hurt, George," she said, "but only for a moment."

She took his arm, and George let out a scream.

"But the needle hasn't touched you yet," said the nurse, laughing.

"There, now it's done. That wasn't so bad, was it?"

No, it really was not. And anyway, it was over now.

—from *Curious George Goes to the Hospital,* by Margaret and H. A. Rey in collaboration with the Children's Hospital Medical Center, Boston

Like Curious George, many children will face a shot, an illness, or a hospital stay. Happily, these exceptional events will be short-lived for them. However, there are children whose problems in areas of health and/or development accrue long-term stress. Mind-body techniques can help youngsters through these short-term and long-term special situations, including:

1. those who are normally healthy but may be undergoing hospitalization or surgery for an acute condition or accident, such as a tonsillectomy or broken arm;
2. those with chronic conditions or illness, such as children with asthma, diabetes, or cancer;
3. those with developmental disabilities, who face challenges of a physical, mental, or emotional nature requiring medical and/or special-education interventions

(these children are frequently called "children with special needs" or "exceptional children");

4. Children who have experienced traumatic events or circumstances, including violence, disaster, or family dysfunction.

The use of mind-body practices with each of these groups of children could require a complete book of its own—and, indeed, books have been written exclusively for them. What follows is an introduction to using mind-body techniques with children in these special situations, and at the end of the chapter we have provided Special Healthgames, primarily for children with special developmental needs, which can be modified to the needs of your child.

However, we have intentionally not included mind-body exercises for children with specific medical conditions, on the advice of pediatricians who teach these techniques to children.

For a number of reasons, it is recommended that parents seek out a health professional to teach mind-body techniques to children with medical conditions such as headaches or asthma, rather than teach them to their own children. The first of these reasons is the risk of misdiagnosing your child's condition. For example, Dr. Karen Olness, professor of pediatrics at Case Western Reserve University, conducted a study of 200 children who were referred to her specifically to learn relaxation/mental imagery strategies. Twenty-five percent of these children were found to have a previously unrecognized, serious biologic basis for their symptoms, ranging from carbon monoxide poisoning to thyroid disease. If your child has recurrent headaches, for example, make sure that she has a thorough medical evaluation.

Once a medical diagnosis, if any, has been made, ask your child's pediatrician or family physician to recommend a clinician qualified to teach relaxation and mental imagery. (A therapist, such as a social worker, psychologist, psychiatrist, or school counselor may also be able to refer you.) Include your child in this process, discussing why you think learning these approaches would help.

Clinicians familiar with mind-body approaches can also be

located through the American Society of Clinical Hypnosis (2200 East Devon Avenue, Suite 291, Des Plaines, IL 60018; 708-297-3317) or through the Society for Clinical and Experimental Hypnosis (315-652-7299).

Working together with a clinician to develop their own exercises allows children to tailor exercises to that child's needs. Dr. Daniel P. Kohen, in the departments of pediatrics and family practice and community health at the University of Minnesota, has helped many children develop their own imagery. He says, "For these techniques to be of most value and use to the individual child, they should only be taught to child patients by their individual clinicians appropriately trained to use these methodologies in the context of their profession."

Olness requests that parents refrain from even *reminding* their children to practice these techniques, especially if the child has a chronic habit or chronic disease. "Many chronically ill children are not in control of much of their treatment," Olness says. "Their self-regulation exercises should belong to them. We offer them at least one method over which they can be in control. This is very important. Children are usually relieved when I say, 'My rule is that your parents cannot remind you to do this, because only you can be in charge of this practice.'"

WHEN YOUR CHILD GOES TO THE HOSPITAL

Day 1

There is a girl in my hospital room who is wearing blue face paint, and she is almost bald. Then this nice nurse came, named Georgette. She took my pulse and blood pressure. Now it's time for a blood test.

"Uh-oh," my roommate, her name is Paige, said.

Later I asked Georgette what Paige has. She says, "Leukemia." I feel bad for her. The chemotherapy made her lose her hair.

For dinner I had macaroni and cheese and vanilla pudding. The macaroni is the worst I have ever tasted.

It's around one in the morning. I just threw up.

It's six in the morning and a nurse just woke me for blood pressure.

The Day

I am really scared. I am being wheeled into the operating room. My parents and I wave good-bye to each other. Something strange has happened. Now that I am in here, I don't feel scared anymore. This doctor who had come to my room yesterday is here. He is the anesthesiologist.

He now puts a mask on my face with sweet-smelling gas and tells me to count. Everything is kind of shaky now. . . . 43 . . . 44 . . . 45. I guess I'll have my tonsils out now. I'm going to close my eyes.

Blink.

I'm at the edge of the table. I have a slight pain in my throat.

"Ah, she woke early," someone says. An orderly comes and wheels me into the recovery room. I feel kind of sleepy. A nurse says I'll see my parents soon.

Here's my Dad.

"Hi, Miss Bumble," my Dad says. "What a trooper! How do you feel?"

"Aaugh," I moan. My throat hurts a little more now.

"So, are you feeling kind of yucky?" a nurse asks.

"Yeah," I try to say. Ouch, that hurt. I can't open my mouth all the way. I want to ask the nurse if she can take off this oxygen mask I've been wearing, but I can't talk.

—*Margie, age ten* (from her hospital journal)

About 4.5 million children are hospitalized each year, and one-third of the children in the United States will be hospitalized at least once before they reach adulthood.

Many aspects of hospitalization—and surgery, in particular—can invoke anxiety, at best, and terror, at worst, in a child. They can include: being in an unfamiliar environment, examined and touched by strangers; getting blood tests, X rays, injections; and, in the case of surgery, being separated from their parents, wheeled into an operating room, being physically restrained, having a mask put over one's face, and waking up in a recovery room with a wound or in pain. These experiences can lead to such problems as nightmares or stuttering later on.

The child may feel powerless, abandoned, or abused, or may be afraid that he or she will die. Some children think they have been sent to the hospital because of something bad they did. Preschool children (under age five) seem most concerned about being separated from their parents, while school-age children are afraid their bodies aren't working right and that they will be different from other kids.

The more information children have, the less frightening hospitalization can be for them. It can be helpful, for example, to tell your child that the operation (or other medical procedure) is for a specific part of the body. If possible, let the child know in advance whether there will be a scar, stitches, or a bandage.

We had a striking experience of the value of information and honesty when Ezra had his sledding accident at age six. The doctors strapped him into a "papoose"—a device to keep him still while they were sewing up the stitches in his forehead. Ezra began to kick within the restraint. "Get me out of this stupid thing!" he cried.

One of the doctors said, "You need to stay in this to keep warm."

A moment later, Ezra shouted, "I'm hot! Get me out of this!"

At this point, we told Ezra that he needed to be in the papoose to keep him still so that the doctors could sew up his wound properly. Seeing the logic of this explanation, Ezra completely calmed down.

Many hospitals prepare children in advance by giving them facts about their hospital stay through puppet shows, films depicting a hospitalized child going through surgery or another medical procedure, playing hospital with dolls, and tours of the hospital.

Some hospitals even give children a ride on a gurney and put an anesthesia mask on the child's face, explaining that the anesthetic will make them feel sleepy.

Studies show that children seven years of age and older benefit from early preparation, whereas younger children should be prepared closer to the time of surgery. The more information a child receives, the less frightening surgery will be. Some hospitals also teach children imagery and relaxation techniques, which by releasing their muscle tension and reducing their upset feelings can decrease pain and medical complications. The children can practice these exercises at home and then do them in the hospital. At one hospital, boys and girls who learned relaxation and imagery techniques from an educational film would calmly roll up their sleeves and offer the surprised lab technician their arms.

You and your child can use any of the relaxation or imagery exercises in this book for this purpose. (*Note:* Because the child's arm may be partially restrained by an IV, exercises that require less physical movement, such as the breathing relaxations or instant relaxation in Chapter 2, may be best.)

Images of water can be very soothing for children. Dr. Lizette Peterson, professor of psychology at the University of Missouri at Columbia, and an expert on child hospitalization, suggests guiding children in visualizing themselves on a raft floating on a lake.

We have also used the following waterfall visualization, which children find very relaxing:

Exercise 9.1   Waterfall Visualization 2–3 min. Ages 6–12. *Goal:* To relax, to relieve feelings of discomfort. (This exercise helped Ezra cope with itching from chicken pox.)

Imagine you are sitting in a cool, green forest at the foot of a refreshing waterfall. Delicious-smelling pine trees and fragrant air surrounds you, and a spray of water from the waterfall sprinkles your back. It feels so good. Soon you move closer to the waterfall, close enough to feel splashed on all the hot, burning parts of your body. Your arms, neck, shoulders, back, and legs feel the cooling splash of water. You sit there a long time. Everything feels cool and clean and delicious, even after you leave the waterfall.

You may want to draw a picture with your favorite colors of the waterfall. You can hang it by your bed and look at it often.

A strategy called stress immunization is similar in theory to vaccinating children against infectious disease, in the sense that stress can be managed in advance, while children are relatively anxiety-free. Stress-immunization activities may include relaxation, desensitization (building up a child's tolerance to stress by introducing the least stressful information first), role-playing (patient plays doctor or nurse, for example), and play activities that familiarize them with hospital equipment. Researchers at the University of California, Los Angeles, School of Nursing, found that stress immunization can successfully reduce the stress of hospitalized children.

Children who are less fearful are more likely to cooperate with diagnostic and other medical procedures. Research shows that speaking to children empathetically can help allay their fears. In one study, for example, a laboratory technician told one group of children having blood tests to be brave and sit still. The technician treated another group of children more empathetically. "I'll bet the alcohol feels cold. In a moment I'm going to stick you. You're probably feeling scared." The children who were told to be brave cried *more* and cooperated *less* than those who were told it was okay to be scared.

Because children respond to sensations differently than adults do, it may be inappropriate to tell them that a needle, for example, may hurt them. "Projection of adult images may engender fears and negative experiences in children," says Dr. Karen Olness of Case Western Reserve University. Olness suggests saying, "This feels different to different people. It might be interesting to imagine a way you could feel comfortable."

Following this advice when our son Zachary began to receive nightly growth-hormone injections, we told him, "Getting a needle feels different to different people at different times. Sometimes it feels cold, sometimes it hurts, sometimes it feels funny, and sometimes it feels other ways. Tell us how it feels." Zach would tell us when the shot hurt, felt wet, and even tickled. And after one shot, Zach said, "It felt nothing."

We also found it helped Zach to have control over *when* he got his shot. We asked Zach to pick a number and when we counted up to that number he would get his shot. Zach picked the number 89. So we counted to 80 by tens and then up to 89 by ones. Sometimes Zach would come up with his own distractions, such as reading a book, playing a video game, or listening to music on a Walkman while he got his shot. (Walkmans are particularly helpful in the hospital, because they can soothe or distract children without disturbing their neighbors.)

Music can help even very young children to relax. A study at Miller's Children's Hospital in Long Beach, California, observed stress behaviors such as crying, throwing objects, body tension, and lethargy among twenty-seven hospitalized infants and toddlers (from five weeks to three years of age). Each of the children was given a music-therapy program, including relaxation, movement, songs, and games with a music therapist, which appeared to reduce the stress behaviors.

At the University of Oklahoma Health Sciences Center, a stress-management program, which included relaxation, breathing, imagery, attention distraction, and rewards, helped relieve the distress of boys undergoing painful medical treatment for their burn injuries.

Similarly, another method, "stress-point" nursing, prepares children and their parents for crucial points of stress during the hospital stay. These include admission and the trip to the recovery room. Studies conducted by Dr. Madelon A. Visintainer, currently chairman of pediatric nursing at Yale University, and her colleagues found that children prepared in this way appear to be less upset during the actual hospital stay than those who don't get stress-point training.

Hospitalization of a child is clearly a major source of stress for parents. Children pick up on their parents' anxiety and stress. A study by Dr. James K. Skipper of the Yale New Haven Medical Center showed that simply reassuring parents by giving them a small amount of factual knowledge dramatically improved the recovery of their children after tonsillectomy. In the study, children having tonsillectomies were divided into two groups. Nurses gave the mothers in one group twenty minutes of explanation

about the operation and what would happen to their child—several minutes on admission, several directly before the operation, and several before going home. Mothers in the second group were given minimal information.

After surgery, children from the first group had lower temperatures (less fever), lower pulse rates, lower blood pressure, were able to urinate sooner, had less nausea and vomiting, drank more fluids, and on the whole had a much faster recovery.

Preparing a child for hospitalization and surgery can have long-term benefits. A study led by Dr. Lizette Peterson at the University of Missouri at Columbia found that children (ages two through ten) who had been prepared for their tonsillectomies using some of the methods mentioned above remembered more positive aspects of their hospital stay than negative ones.

A dramatic case of coping involves Nicole, the daughter of friends of ours. Nicole excelled in all academic areas, is popular and gifted in art, dance, and acting. At age seven complications arising from a severe strep throat infection, Nicole became so ill that her parents had to hospitalize her on Christmas Eve. Over the next bitterly cold weeks, Nicole's respiratory and heart distress worsened. Many specialists in cardiology, pediatrics, and holistic medicine were called in, and all were puzzled and discouraged by Nicole's deteriorating condition. Despite their dire medical predictions, Nicole's parents roused a community of supportive friends and sat with her in her hospital room day and night. There they prayed, meditated, and visualized together, and asked friends to pray whenever and wherever they could. During painful medical procedures and tests, Nicole would also pray and visualize.

Her practices helped her stay off pain medication, which she disliked taking, during many of the invasive procedures. Although she was quite ill for a long time and would need to take antibiotics after her hospitalization was over, she did recuperate and resume her normal life. In Nicole's case, what she did, combined with the family's strong faith and religious values, helped her face the challenges of hospitalization and recovery.

COMMON OR CHRONIC CONDITIONS

Common health conditions such as recurring headaches, sleep problems, or asthma can profoundly affect a child's development. For example, chronic pain can delay young children in reaching their developmental milestones such as walking or toilet training. Illness can also impair children's social development by making them feel separate, different from their peers.

Mind-body techniques, such as relaxation and imagery, can help children with chronic conditions by relieving their pain and anxiety and improving their sense of control over difficult circumstances. For some conditions, including stress disorders such as migraine headaches, stress management may even affect the course of the disease.

Based on his experience as codirector of the Stress Management Clinic at Children's Hospital in Seattle, Dr. William M. Womack has estimated that 85 to 90 percent of children with stress disorders who use mind-body techniques "get better."

Headaches

Migraines and other headaches can interfere with schoolwork and social activities, and when severe can incapacitate a child. Mental imagery can help children to relieve the pain and stress of migraine.

For example, at the University of Washington School of Medicine, Dr. Mark Scott Smith and Dr. Womack reported the case of a nine-year-old boy with migraine headaches who practiced visualization techniques twice a day for fifteen minutes. He began by counting backward from ten to zero. As he did so, he pictured himself walking through a pile of leaves that were blowing away in the wind. Then he imagined different scenes that gave him a feeling of control, such as a battle in which good "Transformers" defeated evil ones. After he had done this exercise for four weeks, the boy's headaches occurred less often, and after six months they stopped.

Research led by Dr. Karen Olness studied the effectiveness of relaxation and mental imagery (using self-hypnosis) for children

with migraines, as compared with the drug propranolol. The children (ages six to twelve) had significantly fewer headaches during the self-hypnosis period, and those who continued to practice self-hypnosis after the study decreased the frequency of their headaches even further.

Asthma

Asthma is one of the most common and stressful chronic illnesses of childhood. Asthma attacks may necessitate visits to the doctor or emergency room, and although they are usually controlled by drugs, can be life-threatening. Breathing difficulties due to asthma cause a child to miss school and may also limit his or her participation in sports and other activities. Not only does asthma lead to stress, but stress may also trigger or exacerbate asthma attacks. For this reason, stress-management techniques may help control these attacks.

Children with asthma who practice relaxation and imagery can boost their self-esteem and increase their sense of control over their asthma. Moreover, there is evidence that these techniques can reduce the frequency and severity of their asthma symptoms.

Dr. Daniel P. Kohen, of the Behavioral Pediatrics Program, Department of Pediatrics, University of Minnesota, for example, has taught children with asthma to visualize the muscles near their airway becoming more relaxed. The children perform progressive relaxation exercises (tightening and releasing their muscles), and then visualize images related to their asthma, such as picturing themselves riding a tiny motorboat through their body and vacuuming up all the mucus in their breathing tubes. Usually, the kids come up with their own images, such as imagining a Pac-Man gobbling the mucus. (Kohen also suggests avoiding the term "asthma attack," because it increases a child's sense of powerlessness against their illness, and saying instead an "episode" or "event" of asthma.)

One study by Dr. Kohen and his colleagues found that 70 percent of asthmatic children who used imagery and relaxation had fewer symptoms, school absences, and emergency room visits

than they had before. These techniques are effective even with preschoolers, as demonstrated by the Preschool Family Asthma Program, sponsored by the Hennepin County, Minnesota, Lung Association and the University of Minnesota Behavioral Pediatrics Program (at that time part of the Minneapolis Children's Medical Center).

Another approach for improving the health and self-esteem of children with asthma is AIR WISE, an individualized education program designed to teach children to manage their own asthma. AIR WISE was created by a group of researchers at the American Institutes for Research in Palo Alto, California.

The Air Wise researchers taught the children coping skills in three areas:

Prevention, which includes controlling emotions that might lead to episodes and "mind-control" techniques to keep them from occurring;

Intervention, such as using relaxation techniques once an episode has begun; and

Modifying behaviors that might affect their illness—for example, avoiding using asthma episodes to manipulate parents and others. Children in the AIR WISE training program had fewer emergency visits than those who received no training.

Several years ago, Deborah, whose then-three-year-old son Russell had asthma, asked Sheila to teach her and Russell some mind-body techniques for managing asthma episodes when they occurred, and ways to relax between these episodes.

Russell's mom and Sheila also included Becky, his older sister, in exercise sessions, as she often felt that her brother was the center of attention in the family because of his asthma. She revealed feelings that are typical of many "healthy" siblings of children who are "fragile," "ill," or "special." While overtly concerned with Russell's condition, Becky's sometimes intrusive domination of Russell (in her mind justifiable) reflected resentment, confusion, and guilt. Becky was given the important job of

drawing the exercises so that she and Russell could practice them between sessions with Sheila.

Movement and massage, imagery and relaxation techniques, along with a lot of Russell's invented games and play, made up the weekly sessions. Becky was right. Russell's asthma did dominate the household in so many ways that seemingly couldn't be helped. It caused his parents anxious and somewhat sleepless nights, and his mother lost days from her job.

By putting it to positive use, the power of his illness was transmuted. In imagery exercises Russell would visualize himself as "Prince Rusty" or some version of a conquering hero. He would embark on rescue missions inside his own body where he would, for instance, sponge up the "gooky asthma stuff" in his lungs with giant sponges. When the sponges became full, he would throw them away. In one session, imaginary play was combined with light-pressure massage work. Sheila applied light pressure to the chest, feet, and so on. Then she showed Russell and his mom exercises such as hatha yoga stretches to balance the energy flow through the body and open up congested areas. Often Russell created his own delightful exercises: arm swings became helicopters, and shoulder shrugs became the "Incredible Hulk" turning into the Hulk from his disguise as an ordinary man.

Over several months, as Russell gained in mastery and control through practicing mind-body techniques, his parents reported fewer hospital emergency room visits and better nighttime sleep. Russell was also having fun while the exercises reduced stress and the effects of his illness. The exercises were incorporated into Russell's life, along with careful diet, herbal medicine, regular medication, and pediatric care. Russell's parents and sister experienced a lessening of asthma's grip on the family.

Diabetes

Diabetes is a chronic illness that when first diagnosed has a major impact on the lifestyle of not only the child with diabetes but that of the entire family. According to Felicia M. Saunders, author of *Your Diabetic Child* and the mother of two diabetic daughters, one approach to helping newly diagnosed diabetic children is for the

parent to follow the same treatment as the diabetic child for one week, observing the same dietary restrictions as the child, and even taking injections with a harmless saline solution. In addition to working closely with the hospital staff and your child's doctor, and going to a support group, this can help you to confront and understand the reality of diabetes' impact on the family, Saunders says. (Discuss the feasibility of this approach with your physician.)

One way to reduce the stress children feel about their diabetes, Saunders adds, is to create an environment in which it is safe to communicate about feelings. The child coming to terms with diabetes needs to be able to express the feelings as they come up. As in the case with children with other chronic conditions, stress-management techniques such as relaxation exercises can be effective.

There is some evidence that relaxation may even affect physiological aspects of non-insulin-dependent diabetes. Consult your child's physician about adding relaxation techniques to your child's regimen.

Cancer

When Erma Bombeck set out to write a book on children with cancer, they told her to change her first chapter. "The first chapter should be 'Am I Gonna Die?' because that's what's everyone thinks about when they're first diagnosed." Children, like adults, with cancer have a life-threatening disease, and that fact can shake up their world.

But children with cancer are still children and can be painfully aware that people who look at them stop seeing a child and see instead a child with cancer. They often have to cope with painful procedures; distressing side effects of treatment, such as nausea, vomiting, and hair loss; and in some cases, a permanent disability (such as the loss of a limb) or disfigurement.

There is, of course, no substitute for the love, sensitivity, and support of families, friends, and caregivers. Mind-body techniques, such as imagery and relaxation, can also help children with cancer by helping them achieve some measure of control over their symptoms and fears. These practices can be enormously

empowering for children in profoundly disempowering circumstances. For example, Dr. Karen Olness found that nineteen of twenty-five children with cancer who learned self-hypnosis (imagery and relaxation) decreased their pain and nausea.

Innovative distraction techniques—to take a child's mind off his or her pain, anxiety, or the anticipatory nausea that can occur as a conditioned response before a chemotherapy treatment—have been tailored to the needs of children with cancer. For example, Dr. Leora Kuttner of Vancouver Children's Hospital has used pop-up books, storytelling, and bubble-blowing. At Memorial Sloan-Kettering Cancer Center in New York, Drs. William Redd, Paul Jacobson, and their colleagues have offered children distractions as high-tech as video games and as low-tech as party blowers. They've also led children in imagery—such as imagining that they're wearing a magic glove that protects them from the pain of a needle puncture.

Imagery can also help children endure painful diagnostic procedures such as lumbar puncture (frequently called spinal tap) and bone-marrow aspiration, during which the child must lie very still while a needle is inserted into the body and a sample (spinal fluid or bone marrow) is drawn. Drs. Lizette Peterson and Cynthia Harbeck, authors of *The Pediatric Psychologist*, have described the way an eight-year-old girl and her mother used imagery to help her undergo a lumbar puncture, as follows:

> Marianne, an eight-year-old girl with cancer, would arrive at the treatment room with her mother. She would take off her wig (her hair had fallen out due to chemotherapy) and her dress, and don a hospital gown. She would position herself on the treatment table, and her mother would hold her hand. Then, together they would create the image of floating on an air mattress on a cool lake, with the warm rays of the sun beating down on her back. She remained calm, motionless, and silent throughout the procedure.

A more controversial use of imagery, which was pioneered by Drs. Carl Simonton and Stephanie Simonton, is imagery of the

immune system—that is, visualizing the white blood cells destroying a cancer cell; or a metaphor for the immune system—picturing a conquering hero such as a knight vanquishing an evil foe. Anecdotal reports suggest that some individuals with cancer who practiced imagery of the immune system—including children—may have survived longer than would have been expected. It is possible, however, that medical treatments, such as chemotherapy or surgery, not imagery, was effective in these cases.

Nevertheless, some people with cancer believe that using imagery in this manner has helped them. Dr. Jimmie C. Holland, chief of psychiatry at Memorial Sloan-Kettering Cancer Center in New York City, believes that patients should be encouraged to practice any technique that helps them to feel better, so long as it does not interfere with their medical treatment and so long as they do not blame themselves for failure should their cancer progress.

Garrett Porter, who at age nine was diagnosed as having an inoperable brain tumor, used imagery of the immune system and other complementary therapies (that is, in addition to standard medical treatment). Together with Dr. Patricia Norris at the Menninger Clinic, Porter used biofeedback and psychosynthesis (a psycho-educational approach to integration of the whole person and the central self) while he received medical treatment. The tumor did eventually disappear. Their account of this complementary and integrative approach is the book *Why Me? Harnessing the Healing Power of the Human Spirit*.

Children with cancer may feel isolated and different from their peers. Interactions with other children who have cancer and reading about the experiences of other young children may help them with these feelings. Jason Gaes, who was diagnosed at age six with Burkitt's lymphoma, a rare cancer, wrote *My book for kids with cansur* when he was eight to help other children with the disease.

Like children in other crisis situations, children with cancer often find the inner resources to endure the most frightening and painful circumstances. As Erma Bombeck writes:

> I never realized how resilient children are—how
> much physical pounding these small bodies can take

and still come up smiling. Just when you think they are lost forever in a swirl of dark waters and rough seas, they surface to bob along innocently awaiting the next assault.

Sadly, not all children with cancer survive their illness. A six-year-old girl we knew, Madeline, died of complications from treatment for a rare form of cancer. Her mother told us she was joyous and loving until the very end. She often asked her mother not to be sad. She spoke of angels, lights, and heaven as if she'd already crossed a threshold from her living world to the next one. At Madeline's memorial service, parents, grandparents, friends, and relatives decided to keep with Madeline's wish "not to be sad." They read poems and sang her favorite hymns and songs.

In the next months, Madeline's mother turned to meditation to deal with her grief and to contact the spirit of joy that her child's life had come to mean to her.

Bedwetting

Most children begin to stay dry at night around the age of three years. However, about 15 percent of children, primarily boys, wet the bed after the age of three. Sometimes bedwetting runs in families, and it usually stops by puberty. Occasional accidents may occur, particularly when a child is ill.

Bedwetting (enuresis) is not a disease but rather a symptom. Bedwetting may be related to a sleep disorder, allergies, a kidney or bladder problem, developmental delay, or emotional problems.

A child may start bedwetting because of new fears or insecurities, such as the arrival of a new baby, moving to a new town, or the loss of a family member. Children usually feel ashamed after bedwetting incidents.

Consult your pediatrician or family physician about your child's bedwetting. If the child also has symptoms of emotional problems—such as persistent sadness or irritability or a change in eating or sleeping habits—ask your physician to refer you to a mental health professional (see "Where to Go for Help" at the end of Chapter 3).

Dry All Night: The Picture Book Technique That Stops Bedwetting, by Alison Mack, describes techniques for stopping bedwetting, including a series of imagery exercises (referred to as seeing a picture of yourself in your head). These include the child visualizing himself as the fire chief having control over the fire truck, or picturing herself getting up out of bed during the night to go to the bathroom. For example, the book encourages children to see themselves as "the boss over your bladder muscle," gives them affirmations such as "you're only going to urinate when you are wide awake," and helps reduce the feeling of shame and isolation by telling them stories about other kids who wet. In one story, a boy is visited by a magic camel who takes him to a place called Dry Land.

DEVELOPMENTAL AND LEARNING DIFFERENCES

If normal childhood is stressful, then children with special needs have an added burden. These children frequently have a cluster of issues in such areas as learning, behavior, socialization, perceptual or motor function, and speech. Some have obvious "abnormal" features, speech, or movements. Yet others, who may look and speak like their peers, have invisible (and even unlabeled or undiagnosed) handicaps that may go undetected by the untrained eye or ear.

A child who has trouble processing and retrieving language, for instance, may have refrained from answering a question not because he is disobedient; he simply can't express himself in the conventional sense. When he does express himself, it may come out at the "wrong" time, in the "wrong" way, and he may be perceived as being "socially incorrect." These children may be blamed for clumsiness; speaking too loudly, softly, or not at all; and for a host of indiscreet behaviors. Their "punishment" is often invisible, too. They are unthinkingly stared at, made fun of, and not invited to parties or included in the regular social events of their peers. Mind-body techniques can help these children develop strong self-esteem and self-concept in the light of extra

demands (schoolwork may be harder for them) and unwitting prejudice.

According to one estimate, approximately 10 to 20 percent of school-age children have trouble with academic work. This includes children with learning difficulties (or who have trouble learning the way their schools teach), and those who have trouble sitting still, paying attention, or controlling their impulses. Feeling like the odd man out, being shamed or teased for "getting in trouble," and/or struggling to stay afloat academically, children with learning or behavior differences are not only under stress, but that stress can also magnify their challenges. So impulsivity, distractibility, hyperactivity, and attention deficits can negatively impact a child's ability to learn, and a child's frustration at finding it hard to learn can lead to troublesome behavior.

These school problems spill over into other arenas, including the family and the child's social life. For example, an impulsive child who has difficulty thinking before speaking, who constantly grabs other kids' stuff, or who calls out in class will have difficulty making and keeping friends or functioning well in the classroom.

There are many interventions available that address particular goals and/or the overall development of the child. We wouldn't presume to tell you what approach would be best for your child, but whichever course of action you elect, we would encourage you to make some form of empowerment available to your child.

Dr. Georgi York Antar, of the Department of Child Psychiatry at Bellevue Hospital, has developed a school-based intervention program for children diagnosed with attention-deficit hyperactivity disorder, using a biobehavioral (or mind-body) approach. The goal of this approach, which includes relaxation, breathing, positive self-talk or reframing, and imagery, is to strengthen the child's inner sense of controls, or inner locus of control. (Locus of control means our sense of where control is located—either internally, that is, within us, or externally, that is, outside of ourselves, as being within other people, situations, etc.) Outer forms of control (such as the use in classrooms of charts, rewards, and demerits) may help manage challenging behaviors,

but often these shifts in behavior do not become transferable to other situations, because they do not become internalized (that is, the behavior change is imposed by the external setting, such as the classroom, rather than coming from or being instilled within the child). In a sense, the child with attention or behavior differences needs to learn to regulate and control his or her impulses from within as well as from without. This sense of inner mastery can start to build self-esteem and self-awareness in a child who typically lacks them.

Breathing, relaxation (such as progressive muscle relaxation), and imagery exercises can impart this sense of mastery. So can role-playing—the child gets to see what her behavior looks like from the outside and can come up with inventive ways to help you (playing her) do something different. So can games such as What Should We Do with This Feeling? (see Chapter 3), in which the child can learn a range of responses instead of his or her usual ones.

Dr. June Groden, director of the Groden Center in Providence, Rhode Island, has said, "Children with special needs probably have more stress and anxiety than other children, so it is important to learn how to reduce and manage their stress."

The Groden Center uses such techniques as relaxation, deep breathing, and imagery with children, adolescents, and adults with autism, mental retardation, and schizophrenia.

Professionals at the Groden Center identify stressful situations and then teach the children to use relaxation at those times. For example, the children may imagine themselves in situations that cause them anxiety. As they imagine they're becoming upset, they can take a deep breath and relax. Relaxation and deep breathing can be helpful for children with behavioral disorders or speech and language problems, including stuttering. These techniques work well with the child's regular therapies (such as speech or physical therapy, and psychotherapy).

Special Healthgames that are helpful to children who have motor, perceptual, attentional, or behavioral problems, including disorders in reading, writing, movement, and speech, appear at the end of this chapter. Of course, these children can also benefit from regular Healthgames tailored to their needs.

Based on the premise that dance and movement facilitate the expression of one's self through one's body, Marybeth Weinstock, a dance and movement educator and therapist, explores emotionality with special-needs kids through creating inner and outer structures. These structures take the form of organized games, free play, and group music and movement activities.

Weinstock suggests that playing a highly structured game with simple-to-understand rules before free play is a way to establish the external and therefore the internal structure. Rhythmic games are helpful, since rhythm is a most basic form of organization and underlies all bodily processes. For instance, children can roll, push, kick, or hit a beach ball to background music or a voice calling out rhythmically "catch and throw."

For children with expressive, neurologic, or psychological difficulties, ball playing "covers many bases." It's fun, requires exertion and propulsion, which are great energy and anger releasers, and teaches children how to mobilize their strength. This empowers them and channels their emotions in a positive way. Ball playing can be as informal as bouncing a large recreational ball back and forth between parent and child.

Working on body image, what Weinstock calls a "three-dimensional mental picture or image a person has of his or her own body" and self-concept, "the emotional feeling one has regarding that image" is the third area of concern. Exercises that lead to children's increased self-awareness and strengthened body image (such as the Bodyspace exercises 5.2 and 5.3 on pp. 91 and 92 in Chapter 5) allow them to relax and interact more appropriately with their environment and the people in it. In turn, they can become better at sharing, handling play materials, and playing cooperatively.

Suzi Tortora-Biederman, a movement-dance therapist, used a similar approach with nursery school children with developmental, emotional, and learning delays. She felt that these children had a hard time proclaiming their "me-ness," who they were as separate individuals in the world, and that music and dance could help them affirm their identities. Because at their age and development, kinesthetic or active learning takes precedence

over verbal learning (according to Tortora-Biederman), the children got the message as they sang and danced. Through movement and music, they learned "who they were."

TRAUMA: MATTERS OF LIFE AND DEATH

We've seen that some events, like having a serious accident, illness, or disability, are enormously traumatic for children. In addition, events that are unforeseen, accidental, unspeakable, and/or shocking belong to the category of trauma we call catastrophic. They range from witnessing a catastrophe—such as the 1993 explosion in the World Trade Center (in which children were trapped for over five hours in an elevator) or the space shuttle *Challenger* explosion—or violent act, to being caught in a life-threatening disaster such as an earthquake or flood, to being the victim of physical or sexual abuse, or losing a loved one.

In his book *Trauma in the Lives of Children*, Dr. Kendall Johnson, a family therapist and crisis-management consultant, classifies childhood traumas into three groups: loss, victimization, and family pathology. Severe loss may include that of a close relative or friend through death or separation, or loss of normal function through illness or injury. Researchers have found that children who have lost a parent tend to have behavioral problems (particularly if the child was younger than five years old when the death occurred), poor school attendance, and high incidence of substance abuse. Children who have lost a parent may need to undergo a healing process to understand and come to terms with the reality and circumstances of the death. Dr. Paul V. Trad, a child psychiatrist at Cornell Medical College, suggested that children who must endure a separation from one or both parents because of divorce or a long workday may also experience a sense of loss that could lead to psychiatric problems and even physical illness.

Victims of crimes or abuse tend to pass through three stages: impact, recoil, and reorganization. During the impact stage, the victim may have emotional symptoms—such as feelings of

helplessness, guilt, shame; or physical symptoms—such as sleep disturbances, loss of appetite, or shortness of breath. During the recoil stage, victims may alternate between focusing obsessively on the event and trying to get on with their lives as if it never happened. During reorganization, the final stage, victims move beyond the event, and feelings such as fear or rage that stem from the event become less intense. However, some traumatic feelings may remain into adulthood. Victims of sexual abuse, particularly, may have long-term feelings of depression, low self-esteem, and guilt.

In groundbreaking research, Dr. Lenore Terr, a California psychiatrist, has found that children who have undergone harrowing experiences may develop post-traumatic stress disorder (PTSD). PTSD consists of continuing emotional and physical consequences such as nightmares, intense fears, personality changes, and flashbacks (replaying the traumatic event in the mind). Combat veterans and rape victims have also suffered from PTSD. For example, in 1976 twenty-three children on their way to summer school in Chowchilla, California, were kidnapped at gunpoint, held hostage, and buried underground before they eventually escaped. Terr noted that fourteen of the twenty-three did, indeed, develop PTSD and were riddled with fears—of the future, of dying, of being kidnapped again, and of losing their parents.

The third type of trauma is family pathology, which can hinder normal development. Researchers have suggested that a dysfunctional family may lead to psychosocial illness in a child—emotional problems in the family either cause a well child to become physically ill or, if the child is already ill, can worsen his condition. One study concluded that children were at greater risk for psychosocial illness if their families were enmeshed (that is, family members were overly involved with one another), overprotective, rigid, and unsuccessful at resolving their conflict.

At least 7 million American children have an alcoholic parent. These children are at greater risk for having emotional problems than children whose parents are not alcoholics, according to the American Academy of Child and Adolescent Psychiatry.

In all of these extreme cases of trauma, extensive, ongoing professional help may not only speed recovery but may be essential for recovery to take place.

SPECIAL HEALTHGAMES

Healthgames may be used for children with special needs, and adapted accordingly. For instance, the muscle-relaxation exercise below might be enhanced for children with physical disabilities, such as cerebral palsy or low muscle tone. Add to the verbal cues of "tense" and "release" rubber squeeze toys or toys that make sounds, such as horns. These toys will make it easier for children with muscular problems to relax, and the sounds will reinforce their efforts. Other exercises can be individualized.

Note: We recommend that you consult the physician and therapists who work with your child regarding the appropriateness of each exercise for her. (They may also be used with siblings and friends of these children.)

Exercise 9.2   Relaxation Preparation and Ready Set Relax 3–10 min. (increase time gradually) Ages 4–7.

Note: The first goal of relaxation preparation is to evaluate a child's ability to follow directions and relax. Then gear each session accordingly.
Goal: To develop concentration. To help a distractible child to focus on an activity. To induce muscle relaxation and learn how to relax completely at will. To use before a medical visit or procedure (or other stressful situations).
1. Ask child to sit still on a chair or couch. Ask her to be as still as a statue, i.e., to "freeze."
2. Have child breathe in and out to a count of four. Now begin relaxation by show and tell. Show child what you mean, while explaining it step by step.
3. Raise your right arm and tighten it. Tighten the hands and fingers. Loosen the arm, hand, and fingers. Shake it out, and rest the arm on top of your right leg.

4. Do the same with the left arm, hand, and fingers.

5. Lift the right foot off the floor about three inches. Circle it to the right and left. Tighten it by pointing the toe, relax it, and plant it down on the floor.

6. Repeat this with the left foot.

7. Tighten the muscles of the neck and face, like this: Stick out your jaw, crinkle up your face. Now open your mouth, make an O, and swivel the O from side to side. Let the jaw relax. Close your mouth. Relax the face by letting it go soft and loose.

8. If you feel any other muscle that is tight or tense, relax it and let it go soft and loose, but not limp.

9. Sit relaxed for a minute, listening to some music or the counting of your breathing, before "unfreezing" and moving about.

Note: Children with special needs may need extra help in relaxing all their muscles while breathing. Parents or other helpers can say slowly or spell out the word "relax" as the children exhale. If this is too difficult, before the relaxation session play with toys that help increase breathing and open up the air flow, such as whistles, harmonicas, bubble sets, pinwheels, pipes, party horns and blowers, and other toys requiring blowing.

Exercise 9.3   Roller Derby 10 min. Ages 5–9.

Goal: To improve balance. To teach body and spatial awareness concepts, especially to children with motor problems. To enhance sense of "body power."

Use skateboards or skates. Best to skate outside or on a wooden floor cleared of obstacles. Play favorite music, and free-skate or introduce concepts such as faster/slower, backward/forward. Children in wheelchairs can use their "wheels."

Exercise 9.4   Ball Playing 10 min. Ages 4–12.

Goal: To teach use of objects in space, which in turn helps social relationships, gross motor skills such as aim and propulsion, and hand-eye and eye-foot coordination. When these skills are learned, self-esteem and confidence improve.

🌿 Choose the size and bounceability of a ball in accordance with the child's size and development, with bigger, bouncier balls for smaller children. Establish a rhythm through use of a catchy chant, such as "Way to go, way to go!" or music. Then keep your eyes on the ball, by bouncing, kicking, hitting, and throwing back and forth among players. Devise a point or team system, or play free ball.

Exercise 9.5 Worthy Words Untimed. Ages 2 and up.
Goal: To integrate "speech games" into home, using sibling of special-needs child as "helper." To stimulate speech and language development for all children. To enhance self-concept through praise.

🌿 For children who are just learning to talk, this is a game to reward language use. Make a chart and place a star next to any new word used correctly (or coming close). Have older child play with younger.

A variation on worthy words for older children or children with speech problems: Write notes of praise with difficult or new vocabulary, and stick to child's dresser or desk, such as: "You were so considerate in sharing your toys with brother," or "Thank you for your exquisite table manners at dinner."

Exercise 9.6 Clay Play; Playdough Untimed. Ages 4–8.
Goal: Creative expression. To develop hand strength and stability (decrease tremors associated with muscular problems). As there are many therapeutic uses for clay play, individual goals can be set by and with teacher or therapist, and parent.

🌿 1. Explore the world of form and body. Make the people by rolling the shapes of limbs, head, and body parts. Then attach together.
2. Create 3-D letters and numbers. For instance, roll ten snakes and count them, or make a "1" and "0" for the number ten. Tactile or kinesthetic learning is beneficial to all children (as we've seen), especially those with sensory, motor, or learning problems; it reinforces 2-D learning, which is primarily visual.

3. Design a food fest. Using any cutters or shaping forms, make cookies, pizzas, vegetables, burgers, or any other food you like.
   Reinforces "kitchen skills" while helping in naming things.

Exercise 9.7   Simple Simon, Follow the Leader, and other games of direction Untimed. Ages 4–8.
Goal: To develop good listening skills, motor planning.

Following directions is hard for special-needs children, who may have difficulty in either motor planning or paying attention. These games reinforce listening to and following one- or two-step commands. They also give child who is "it" a sense of power and control. Lay out the ground rules as to how you pick leaders, and the hows and whys of "you're out." Emphasize "these are the rules for this game. We can make up our own game another time" over "making up our own rules."

Exercise 9.8   The Hand Walk or Wheelbarrow 1–2 min. Ages 3–7.

Goal: To strengthen muscles, focus concentration.

Adult or partner holds child by the ankles while child walks on hands to destination, wheelbarrow style. This is a great activity for older and younger siblings. Add music, timers, or obstacles (for example, walk over the shoe or the block).

Exercise 9.9   Opposites Game 5 min. Ages 5–10.
Goal: To develop kinesthetic awareness, coordination. Assists children with learning disabilities or speech and/or hearing impairment in self-expression and communication.

🌿 In this dance game, children act out pairs of opposites with their bodies, such as short-tall, backward-forward, slow-fast. Can be done to live or taped music, or to a rhythmic drumbeat. Eventually these pairs can be expanded to characters, such as "a fierce, hungry lion and a scared lamb hiding from the lion," or "Peter Pan and Captain Hook."

Variation: The Same Game, where children pair up and one leads and the other follows. The follower mirrors or copies the leader. For children who often "feel" different, acting the "same" is reassuring.

Exercise 9.10 Sticks and Bones 5 min. Ages 5–10.

Similar to Bodyspace exercises (see page 91) with the addition of props.

Goal: To teach spatial awareness and body boundaries.

🌿 Each child stands in a marked-off square. Music begins, and a leader directs the children around, saying, for instance, "Skip forward," "Take three giant steps to the right . . . but don't touch anyone and don't cross anyone's line." The directions should be very specific so that children know exactly what to do. Props to add include: overturned pails or buckets as "towers" for children to walk and dance around, Hula Hoops (to form circle boundaries on the ground), sticks (you can pretend they're bones), blocks (as "buildings" of all kinds), and anything else that allows children to relate to objects, space, and boundaries. By calling sticks names of bones (elbow bone, backbone), you increase vocabulary and knowledge of body parts. Calling Hula Hoops "moats" or "rivers" also builds vocabulary, by teaching children synonyms or "likes."

After children play comfortably with the boundaries, leader can remove props one by one, and regular "Bodyspace" can be played. Children are now encouraged to move more in relation to each other than in relation to the objects.

Epilogue:

Bringing Healthgames Home

By doing practices that help bring our mind-body-spirit into harmony, we can touch upon new dimensions of our personality and self, as we watch our children grow and move from milestone to milestone, eventually crossing the threshold from childhood to adolescence.

1. Practice Healthgames. Start simply, with one or two exercises that seem most compatible with your children's (and your) taste, temperament, skills, and needs—of course, those needs may always be changing. And don't second-guess your kids—they might surprise you. You may think your superactive children would never sit still for meditation, but they might enjoy the sense of focus and mindfulness they gain from it.
2. Don't awfulize. Awesomize.
3. Remember the three C's of hardiness: *Commitment*—stick to your values. *Control*—see yourself as someone who makes things happen instead of as someone things happen to. *Challenge*—see problems as challenges.
4. Practice let-go-ability. Don't get stuck.
5. Keep in touch with your self and stay connected to others.

6. Be helpful. Perform acts of kindness.
7. Find times in the day to move and times to be still. Take a stretch break, for example.
8. Give someone a back rub or a tickle.
9. Find true heroes in real life and in great books and stories.
10. Understand and appreciate other people's differences. Build on your strengths and work on your weaknesses.
11. Remember to breathe, relax, and reward yourself for being a positive child (or adult!).

We encourage you and your children to come up with your own healthgames—kids are particularly creative in the area of visualization, for instance. We would like to hear from you about how you've brought healthgames into your home. Please send us your suggestions and experiences. We welcome one sentence, a paragraph, a picture, a poem, or an essay about something positive in your life.

Write to us c/o: *Stress-Proofing Your Child*, Bantam Books.

Wishing you and your family good health and good spirits.

Sheldon Lewis
Sheila Kay Lewis

Appendix

We have read and learned from hundreds of books in the course of writing *Stress-Proofing Your Child* and have listed the titles of many of these books here. However, the list is by no means complete. We recommend that you visit bookstores and look in the sections on self-help/psychology, mind-body health, spirituality and consciousness, creativity, education and learning, parenting, children's literature, and New Age.

FOR FURTHER READING

Mind-Body Health and Techniques

Benson, Herbert. *The Relaxation Response.* Morrow, New York, 1975.

Benson, Herbert, and Stuart, Eileen M. *The Wellness Book: The Comprehensive Guide to Maintaining Health and Treating Stress-Related Illness.* Simon & Schuster, New York, 1992.

Borysenko, Joan. *Minding the Body, Mending the Mind.* Bantam Books, New York, 1988.

Cousins, Norman. *Anatomy of an Illness.* Norton, New York, 1979.

Gillet, Richard. *Change Your Mind, Change Your World: A Practical Guide to Turning Limiting Beliefs into Positive Realities.* Simon & Schuster, New York, 1992.

Goleman, Daniel, and Gurin, Joel, Eds. *Mind/Body Medicine.* Consumer Reports Books, Yonkers, New York, 1993.

Kabat-Zinn, Jon. *Full Catastrophe Living.* Delacorte, New York, 1990.

Locke, Steven E., and Culligan, Douglas. *The Healer Within.* New American Library, New York, 1986.

Moskowitz, Reed C. *Your Healing Mind.* Morrow, New York, 1992.

Murdock, Maureen. *Spinning Inward.* Shambhala, Boston, 1987.

Ornish, Dean. *Dr. Dean Ornish's Program for Reversing Heart Disease.* Random House, New York, 1990.

Pelletier, Kenneth R. *Sound Mind, Sound Body: A New Model for Lifelong Health.* Simon & Schuster, New York, 1994.

Rossman, Martin L. *Healing Yourself.* Walker & Co., New York, 1987.

Samuels, Mike, and Samuels, Nancy. *Seeing with the Mind's Eye: The History, Techniques, and Uses of Visualization.* Random House, New York, 1975.

Samuels, Mike, and Samuels, Nancy. *The Well Child Book.* Summit Books, New York, 1982.

Williams, Redford. *The Trusting Heart: Great News About Type A Behavior,* especially Chapter 9, "Let's Have More Trusting Children." Times Books, New York, 1989.

Helping Your Child Cope with Stress

Brazelton, T. Berry. *Families: Crisis and Caring.* Addison-Wesley, Reading, Massachusetts, 1989.

Chess, Stella, and Thomas, Alexander. *Know Your Child: An Authoritative Guide for Today's Parents.* Basic Books, New York, 1987.

Elkind, David. *The Hurried Child.* Addison-Wesley, Reading, Massachusetts, 1988.

Feiner, Joel, and Yost, Graham. *Taming Monsters, Slaying Dragons:*

The Revolutionary Family Approach to Overcoming Childhood Fears and Anxieties. Arbor House, New York, 1988.

Nowicki, Stephen, and Duke, Marshall P. *Helping the Child Who Doesn't Fit In*. Peachtree, Atlanta, 1992.

Robinson, Bryan E., Rowland, Bobbie H., and Coleman, Mick. *Home Alone Kids: The Working Parent's Complete Guide to Providing the Best Care for Your Child*. Free Press, New York, 1990.

Seligman, Martin E.P. *Learned Optimism*. Alfred A. Knopf, New York, 1991.

Wallerstein, Judith S., and Blakeslee, Sandra. *Second Chances: Men, Women, and Children a Decade after Divorce*. Ticknor & Fields, New York, 1989.

Weston, Denise Chapman, and Weston, Mark S. *Playful Parenting: Turning the Dilemma of Discipline into Fun and Games*. Jeremy P. Tarcher/Putnam, New York, 1993.

Youngs, Bettie B. *Stress and Your Child: Helping Kids Cope with the Strains and Pressures of Life*. Fawcett Columbine, New York, 1995.

"The Real Me"—Spirituality and Meditation

Burnett, Frances Hodgson. *The Secret Garden*. Bantam, Dell/Yearling Books, New York, 1987.

Kabat-Zinn, Jon. *Wherever You Go There You Are: Mindfulness Meditation in Everyday Life*. Hyperion, New York, 1994.

Luvmour, Sambhava and Josette. *Consciousness, Evolution and Spirituality in Children*. A Holistic Appreciation of Natural Learning Rhythms of Children. c/o Pathfinders/CEG, PO Box 445, North San Juan, California 95960. (916) 292-1000.

Muktananda, Swami. *I Am That*. SYDA Foundation, South Fallsburg, New York, 1978.

Muktananda, Swami. *Meditate*. State University of New York Press, Albany, © 1980, 1991, SYDA Foundation, South Fallsburg, New York.

Rozman, Deborah. *Meditation for Children*. Aslan Publishing, 1989.

Rozman, Steven M. *Spiritual Parenting*. Quest Books, 1994.

Learning and Education

Armstrong, Thomas. *Awakening Your Child's Natural Genius*. Jeremy P. Tarcher, Los Angeles, 1991.

Canfield, Jack, and Wells, Harold. *One Hundred Ways to Enhance Self-Concept in the Classroom*. Resource Center for Redesigning Education, Brandon, Vermont, 1994.

DePorter, Bobbi, with Hernacki, Mike. *Quantum Learning: Unleashing the Genius in You*. Dell Publishing, New York, 1992.

Devenceni, Jane, and Prendergast, Susan. *Belonging: Self and Social Discovery for Children of All Ages*. Resource Center for Redesigning Education, Brandon, Vermont, 1994.

Ellison, Launa. *Seeing with Magic Glasses: A Teacher's View from the Front Line of the Learning Revolution*. Great Ocean Publishers, Arlington, Virginia, 1993.

Gardner, Howard. *Multiple Intelligences: The Theory in Practice*. Basic Books, New York, 1993.

Gardner, Howard. *To Open Minds*. Basic Books, New York, 1989.

Gardner, Howard. *The Unschooled Mind: How Children Think & How Schools Should Teach*. Basic Books, New York, 1991.

Goleman, Daniel. *Emotional Intelligence*. Bantam Books, New York, 1995.

Keirsey, David, and Bates, Marilyn. *Please Understand Me: Character and Temperament Types*. Prometheus Nemesis Books, 1978.

Kline, Peter. *The Everyday Genius: Restoring Children's Natural Joy of Learning—And Yours Too*. Great Ocean Publishers, Arlington, Virginia, 1988.

Lazear, David. *Seven Pathways of Learning: Teaching Parents and Students About Multiple Intelligences*. Zephyr Press, Tucson, Arizona.

Luvmour, Josette and Sambhava. *Natural Learning Rhythms: How and When Children Learn*. Celestial Arts, Berkeley, California, 1993.

Rich, Dorothy. *Megaskills*. Houghton Mifflin, New York, 1992.

Rose, Colin. *Accelerated Learning*, 4th ed. Accelerated Learning Systems Ltd., Aylesbury, Bucks, England, 1989.

Body-Mind Fitness

Benzwie, Teresa. *A Moving Experience: Dance for Lovers of Children and the Child Within.* Zephyr Press, Tucson, Arizona.

Fraser, Diane Lynch. *Playdancing: Discovering and Developing Creativity in Young Children.* Princeton Book Co. Publishers (A Dance Horizons Book), 1991.

Herman, Gail Neary, and Hollingsworth, Patricia. *Kinetic Kaleidoscope: Activities for Exploring Movement and Energy in the Visual Arts.* Zephyr Press, Tucson, Arizona.

Huang, Chungliang Al. *Thinking Body, Dancing Mind: TaoSports for Extraordinary Performances in Athletics, Business, and Life.* Bantam Books, New York, 1992.

Mordden, Ethan. *Pooh's Workout Book.* Penguin Books, New York, 1985.

Sachs, Michael H. Exercise for Stress Control. *Mind/Body Medicine.* Daniel Goleman and Joel Gurin, eds. Consumer Reports Books, Yonkers, New York, 1993, pp. 315–327.

Self-Improvement and Helping Others

Bloch, Douglas. *Words That Heal: Affirmations and Meditations for Daily Living.* Bantam Books, New York, 1990.

Bloch, Douglas, with Merrit, Jon. *Positive Self-Talk for Children. Teaching Self-Esteem Through Affirmations: A Guide for Parents, Teachers, and Counselors.* Bantam Books, New York, 1993.

Cameron, Julia, and Bryan, Mark. *The Artist's Way: A Spiritual Path to Higher Creativity.* Jeremy P. Tarcher/Putnam, New York, 1992.

Covey, Stephen R. *The Seven Habits of Highly Effective People: Powerful Lessons in Personal Change.* Fireside Books/Simon & Schuster, New York, 1989.

Luks, Allan, with Payne, Peggy. *The Healing Power of Doing Good.* Ballantine Books, New York, 1991.

Luvmour, Sambhava and Josette. *Towards Peace. Cooperative Games & Activities.* Available from: Center for Educational

Guidance, Box 445, North San Juan, California, 95960; (916) 292-3623. 1989.

Newman, Fred, and Phyllis Goldberg. *Let's Develop! A Guide to Continuous Personal Growth*. Castillo Intl., New York, 1994.

Heroes and Role Models, from Myth to Media

Campbell, Joseph. *The Hero with a Thousand Faces*. Princeton University Press, Princeton, New Jersey, 1972.

Oppenheim, Joanne, and Oppenheim, Stephanie. *The Best Toys, Books & Videos for Kids*. (Also includes special-needs products.) HarperCollins Publishers, New York, 1995.

Pearson, Carol S. *Awakening the Heroes Within: Twelve Archetypes to Help Us Find Ourselves and Transform Our World*. HarperCollins Publishers, New York, 1991.

Pearson, Carol S. *The Hero Within: Six Archetypes We Live By*. HarperCollins Publishers, New York, 1989.

Special Situations

The Association for the Care of Children's Health has a wealth of information for hospitalized children and their families, including a Pediatric Bill of Rights (your child's rights in the hospital). Contact them as early as possible prior to your child's hospitalization at: 7910 Woodmont Avenue, Suite 300, Bethesda, MD 20814; (301) 654-6549.

Cautela, Joseph R., and Groden, June. *Relaxation: A Comprehensive Manual for Adults, Children, and Children with Special Needs*. Research Press Company, Champaign, Illinois, 1978.

Chaney, Sky, and Fisher, Pam, Eds. *The Discovery Book: A Helpful Guide for the World Written by Children with Disabilities*, revised edition. United Cerebral Palsy of the North Bay, Santa Rosa, California, 1989.

Fine, Judylaine. *Afraid to Ask: A Book for Families to Share About Cancer*. Lothrop, Lee & Shepard Books, New York, 1986.

Gaes, Jason. *My book for kids with cansur: A Child's Autobiography of Hope*, illustrated by Tim and Adam Gaes. Melius & Peterson Publishing, Aberdeen, South Dakota, 1987.

Lobato, Debra J. *Brothers, Sisters, and Special Needs. Information and Activities for Helping Young Siblings with Chronic Illnesses and Developmental Disabilities.* Paul H. Brookes, Baltimore, 1990.

Mack, Alison. *Dry All Night: The Picture Book Technique That Stops Bedwetting.* Little, Brown and Company, Boston, 1989.

Moynihan, Patricia M., and Haig, Broatch. *Whole Parent, Whole Child: A Parent's Guide to Raising a Child with a Chronic Illness.* Chronimed, 1989.

Porter, Garrett, and Norris, Patricia. *Why Me? Harnessing the Healing Power of the Human Spirit.* Stillpoint Publishing, Walpole, New Hampshire, 1985.

Turecki, Stanley, with Tonner, Leslie. *The Difficult Child.* Bantam Books, New York, 1989.

Turecki, Stanley, and Wernick, Sarah. *The Emotional Problems of Normal Children: How Parents Can Understand and Help.* Bantam Books, New York, 1994.

PERIODICALS

There are numerous magazines, including *Child, Parents, Parenting,* and others, that offer advice and features on a wide variety of topics of interest. We list here those that may be harder to find at newsstands, and that specifically cover holistic and mind-body topics:

Holistic Education Review, P.O. Box 328, Brandon, VT 05733; (800) 639-4122.

Mothering, P.O. Box 1690, Santa Fe, NM 87504; (505) 984-8116.

MUSIC

Music that may be helpful for relaxation or meditation:

The Narada Collection Series, including *Earthsongs* and other tapes, available from Friends of Narada, 1845 N. Farwell Ave., Milwaukee, WI 53202; tel.: (414) 272-6700.

Kyrie, Gloria by Wings of Song and Robert Gass, and other tapes
    from Spring Hill Music, P.O. Box 800, Boulder, CO 80306.
Moonglow and other tapes by Daniel Kobialka, from Li-Sem En-
    terprises, 1775 Old Country Rd., #9, Belmont, CA 94002.
Sounds of Light and other tapes are available from: SYDA Founda-
    tion Bookstores, P.O. Box 600, South Fallsburg, NY 12779,
    or tel.: (914) 434-2000, ask for "O" or ext. 7870.
The music of Paul Winter, Steve Halpern, and others are available
    at New Age bookstores or record stores.

Music for learning:

The OptimaLearning® Company has developed a series of tapes
designed to improve concentration, learning, and thinking skills.
These tapes include:

Baroque Music for Learning & Relaxation, vols. 1 and 2; 3 and 4.

Music for Optimal Performance, vols. 1 and 2

Music for Imagination & Creativity, vols. 1 and 2

These tapes and other instructional material are available
from: Barzak Educational Institute International and The Opti-
maLearning Co. 885 Olive Ave., Suite A, Novato, CA 94945;
tel.: (800) 672-1717 (outside CA) or (415) 898-0013.
    Any popular children's artists your child likes enhance relax-
ation and creativity. As mentioned in Chapter 5, a nice exposure
to world cultures, *Sheaves of Grain: Songs from Around the World*, is
available from: The Vanaver Caravan, c/o 298 Mountain Road,
Rosendale, NY 12472.

Some of our family's favorite music includes:

Pachelbel's *Canon in D major/Greatest Baroque Hits*, CBS Master-
    works
Music of Antonio Vivaldi, such as *The Four Seasons*
Bach's Brandenburg concertos
Beethoven's symphonies
Tchaikovsky's *The Nutcracker* and other ballets

ORGANIZATIONS

American Academy of Child and Adolescent Psychiatry
3615 Wisconsin Ave., NW
Washington, DC 20016-3007
(202) 966-7300; fax: (202) 966-2891
Facts for Families—information packets on a wide range of family and parenting issues—are available.

Boulder Center for Emotional and Social Learning
c/o Mediator's Foundation
3833 North 57th Street
Boulder, CO
Shelley Kessler conducts trainings for educators. Her "Mysteries Sourcebook" and videotape about the Mysteries program are available by calling: 1-800-639-4122, "Great Ideas in Education" to order.

The Collaborative for the Advancement of Social and Emotional
    Learning
Yale Child Study Center
P.O. Box 207900
230 South Frontage Road
New Haven, CT 06520-7900
(203) 785-6107; fax: (203) 785-6106
A clearinghouse to help educators contact social and emotional learning programs and resources for use in their own schools.

The Educational Initiatives/Mind-Body Medical Institute
New England Deaconess Hospital
185 Pilgrim Road
Boston, MA 02215
(617) 632-9525
Provides "Life Management Skills" training for teachers and other professionals to learn how to use meditation, relaxation, and other techniques in teaching youth and in coping with their own "burnout." Pilot programs in schools in Boston, Newark, and Los Angeles.

Educators for Social Responsibility (ESR)
Resources for Empowering Children
23 Garden Street
Cambridge, MA 02138
(617) 492-1764
Books, tapes, and institutes on conflict resolution, social responsibility, diversity education, violence prevention, and character development are listed in their catalog.

Family Development Center
The East Side Center for Social Therapy
500 Greenwich St., Suite 201-202
New York, NY 10013
(212) 941-8844
An innovative approach to child and family development. Classes and workshops, as well as children's, family, and parenting groups, are available, with an emphasis on dynamic development, social therapy, and Vygotskian theory. For information about centers in other cities, call the New York office.

The John E. Fetzer Institute
1292 West KL Avenue
Kalamazoo, MI 49009
(616) 375-2000; fax: (616) 372-2163
A leader in mind/body/spirit research and education. Publishes the quarterly journal Advances.

The Institute of Noetic Sciences
475 Gate 5 Road
Suite 300
Sausalito, CA 94965
Research and education focusing on mind-body interactions and human consciousness. Areas of interest include creative altruism, spontaneous remission of illness, and psychoneuroimmunology. Publishes Noetic Sciences Review, *a quarterly journal.*

Insight Meditation Society, Pleasant Street, Barre, MA 01005. Family and adolescent meditation retreats.

Omega Institute, 260 Lake Drive, Rhinebeck, NY 12572; (800) 944-1001. Holistic Education Center, with programs including an annual Family Week.

SYDA Foundation, P.O. Box 600, South Fallsburg, NY 12779; (914) 434-2000. Ongoing classes and programs focusing on meditation, yoga, and related topics, with children's, teen, and family programs.

Selected Bibliography

Introduction

Remen, Rachel Naomi. Feeling Well: A Clinician's Casebook. *Advances* 6:1, 1989.

Chapter 1: Stressbusters

Marcus Aurelius. *Marcus Aurelius Meditations*. Maxwell Staniforth, trans. Penguin Classics, London, 1964.

Benson, Herbert. *The Relaxation Response*. William Morrow & Co., New York, 1975.

Benson, Herbert, and Borysenko, Joan Z. The Relaxation Response and Relaxation Techniques. *Mind-Body-Health Digest* 2:2, 1988.

Borysenko, Joan. *Minding the Body, Mending the Mind*. Bantam Books, New York, 1988.

Cousins, Norman. *Anatomy of an Illness as Perceived by the Patient*. Norton, New York, 1979.

Goleman, Daniel, and Gurin, Joel. *Mind/Body Medicine*. Consumer Reports Books, Yonkers, New York, 1993.

Graham, Barbara. The Healing Power of Humor. *Mind-Body-Health Digest* 4:2, 1990.

Graham, Barbara. The Medicine of Art. *Mind-Body-Health Digest* 4:1, 1990.

Kabat-Zinn, Jon. *Full Catastrophe Living*. Delacorte, New York, 1990.

Lewis, Sheldon. The Whole Child. *Mind-Body-Health Digest* 3:1, Institute for the Advancement of Health, San Francisco, 1989.

Locke, Steven E., and Colligan, Douglas. *The Healer Within*. New American Library, New York, 1986.

Meyer, Roger, and Haggerty, Robert J. Streptococcal Infections in Families. *Pediatrics*, April 1962, 539–549.

Moskowitz, Reed C. *Your Healing Mind*. Morrow, New York, 1992.

Murdock, Maureen. *Spinning Inward*. Shambhala, Boston, 1987.

Murphy, Michael, and White, Rhea A. *The Psychic Side of Sports*. Addison-Wesley, Reading, Massachusetts, 1978.

Nicklaus, Jack. *Golf My Way*. Simon & Schuster, New York, 1974, pp. 79–80 (cited in Murphy and White, *The Psychic Side of Sports*).

Ornish, Dean. *Dr. Dean Ornish's Program for Reversing Heart Disease*. Random House, New York, 1990.

Ornstein, Robert, and Sobel, David. *Healthy Pleasures*. Addison-Wesley, Reading, Massachusetts, 1989.

Rossman, Martin L. *Healing Yourself: A Step-by-Step Program to Better Health Through Imagery*. Walker & Co., New York, 1987.

Rossman, Martin L. Imagery. *How Your Mind Affects Your Health*. Institute for the Advancement of Health, San Francisco, 1990.

Samuels, Mike, and Samuels, Nancy. *Seeing with the Mind's Eye: The History, Techniques, and Uses of Visualization.* Random House, New York, 1975.

The Yellow Emperor's Classic of Internal Medicine. Ilza Veith, ed. University of California Press, 1972.

Wu, Zhao Z. Ch'i Kung. *The Traditional Chinese Breathing Exercises.* Intl. Cultural Services and Trading Co., New York, 1993.

Chapter 2: "Stress Is When You're Having a Rough Time"

American Academy of Child and Adolescent Psychiatry, Facts for Families. 3615 Wisconsin Avenue NW, Washington, DC 20016.

Coles, Robert. *The Spiritual Life of Children.* Houghton Mifflin, Boston, 1990.

Daurora, Dianna L., and Fimian, Michael J. Dimensions of Life and School Stress Experienced by Young People. *Psychology in the Schools.* Jan. 1988, 25:(1) 44–53.

Elkind, David. *The Hurried Child.* Addison-Wesley, Reading, Massachusetts, 1988.

Furman, Erna. What Nursery School Teachers Ask Us About. Psychoanalytic Consultations in Preschools: Stress in the Nursery School. *Emotions and Behavior Monographs,* 1986, Monograph No. 5, pp. 53–68.

Gardner, Howard. *Multiple Intelligences: The Theory in Practice.* Basic Books, New York, 1993.

Gardner, Howard. *To Open Minds.* Basic Books, New York, 1989.

Gardner, Howard. *The Unschooled Mind: How Children Think & How Schools Should Teach.* Basic Books, New York, 1991.

Kuczen, Barbara. *Childhood Stress: Don't Let Your Child Be a Victim.* Delacorte, New York, 1982.

Lewis, Sheldon. Families and Stress: An Interview with T. Berry Brazelton. *Advances* 6(4):34, 1989.

McLoyd, Vonnie C., and Wilson, Leon. Maternal Behavior, Social Support, and Economic Predictors of Distress in Children. In *Economic Stress: Effect on Family Life and Child Development*, McLoyd, Vonnie C., and Flanagan, Constance A., eds. New Directions for Child Development, no. 46. Jossey-Bass, Inc., San Francisco, 1990.

Mind-Body Fitness. *Mind-Body-Health Digest* 3:2, 1989.

Murphy, Michael, and White, Rhea A. *The Psychic Side of Sports*. Addison-Wesley, Reading, Massachusetts, 1978.

O'Reilly, Brian. Why Grade "A" Execs Get an "F" as Parents. *Fortune*, January 1, 1990.

Packard, Vance. *Our Endangered Children: Growing Up in a Changing World*. Little, Brown, Boston, 1983.

Robinson, Bryan E., Rowland, Bobbie H., and Coleman, Mick. *Home Alone Kids: The Working Parent's Complete Guide to Providing the Best Care for Your Child*. Free Press, New York, 1990.

Salk, Dr. Lee. *Familyhood: Nurturing the Values That Matter*. Simon & Schuster, New York, 1992.

Samuels, Mike, and Samuels, Nancy. *The Well Child Book*. Summit Books, New York, 1982.

Spock, Benjamin. *Dr. Spock on Parenting*. Simon & Schuster, New York, 1988, p. 23.

Winn, Marie. *The Disappearance of Childhood*, Pantheon Books, New York, 1983.

Chapter 3: Milestones and Millstones

Brazelton, T. Berry. *Families: Crisis and Caring*. Addison-Wesley, Reading, Massachusetts, 1989.

Brody, Jane E. Children of Divorce; Steps to Help Can Hurt. *New York Times*, July 23, 1991, p. C1.

Erikson, Erik H. *Childhood and Society*, 35th anniversary edition. Norton, New York, 1985.

Feiner, Joel, and Yost, Graham. *Taming Monsters, Slaying Dragons: The Revolutionary Family Approach to Overcoming Childhood Fears and Anxieties*. Arbor House, New York, 1988.

Fraiberg, Selma. *The Magic Years*. Charles Scribner's Sons, New York, 1959.

Heisel, J. Stephen. The Significance of Life Events as Contributing Factors in the Diseases of Children. *Pediatrics* 83:119, 1983.

Holmes, Thomas H., and Rahe, Richard H. The Social Readjustment Rating Scale. *Journal of Psychosomatic Research* 11:213–18, 1967.

Kellerman, Dr. Jonathan. *Helping the Fearful Child: A Parent's Guide*. Warner Books and W. W. Norton & Co. New York, 1981.

Wallerstein, Judith S., and Blakeslee, Sandra. *Second Chances: Men, Women, and Children a Decade after Divorce*. Ticknor & Fields, New York, 1989.

Wickramasekera, Ian. Risk Factors Leading to Chronic Stress-Related Symptoms. *Advances* 4(1):9–35, 1987.

Chapter 4: Discovering the Real Me

Burnett, Frances Hodgson. *The Secret Garden*. Bantam, Dell/Yearling Books, New York, 1987.

Discourse of Vegetable Roots (Ming Dynasty), Chao Tze-chiang, trans. *A Chinese Garden of Serenity: Epigrams from the Ming Dynasty*. Peter Pauper Press, Mount Vernon, 1959.

Dubos, Rene. *The God Within*. Scribner's, New York, 1972.

Emerson, Ralph Waldo. *Journals 1836–38.* Journals and Miscellaneous notebooks. Gilman, William H., et al., eds. Belknap Press of Harvard University Press, Cambridge, 1960.

Goleman, Daniel. *The Meditative Mind.* Jeremy P. Tarcher, Los Angeles, 1988.

Kabat-Zinn, Jon. *Wherever You Go There You Are: Mindfulness Meditation in Everyday Life.* Hyperion, New York, 1994.

Kaplan, Aryeh. *Jewish Meditation.* Schocken Books, New York, 1985.

London, Peter. *No More Secondhand Art: Awakening the Artist Within.* Shambhala, Boston, 1989.

Muktananda, Swami. *I Am That.* SYDA Foundation, South Fallsburg, New York, 1978.

Muktananda, Swami. *Meditate.* SYDA Foundation, State University of New York Press, Albany, 1980, 1991.

Smith, G. Richard, Jr. *Archives of Internal Medicine*, 1985.

Thurman, Howard. *Disciplines of the Spirit.* Harper & Row, New York, 1972, pp. 96–97.

Chapter 5: Body-Mind Fitness

Cottingham, John T. *Healing Through Touch: A History and a Review of the Physiological Evidence.* Rolf Institute, Boulder, Colorado, 1987.

Glasser, William. *Positive Addictions.* Harper & Row, New York, 1976.

Goleman, Daniel. The Experience of Touch: Research Points to a Critical Role. *New York Times*, February 2, 1988.

King, Billie Jean, with Chapin, Kim. *Billie Jean.* Harper & Row, 1974.

Kline, Peter. *The Everyday Genius: Restoring Children's Natural Joy*

of Learning—And Yours Too. Great Ocean Publishers, Arlington, Virginia, 1988.

Liedloff, Jean. *The Continuum Concept: Allowing Human Nature to Work Successfully*. Addison-Wesley, New York City, 1975 original printing, revised edition, 1993.

Mind-Body Education. *Mind-Body Health Digest* 4:2, 1990.

Mordden, Ethan. *Pooh's Workout Book*. Penguin Books, New York, 1985.

Munzenrider, Steven; Newmann, Dana; Coffey, David; DaSilva, Maria; and Stidhiam, Martin. *Little Earth School: Education, Discovery, Celebration*. Schocken Books, New York, 1986.

Murphy, Michael, and White, Rhea A. *The Psychic Side of Sports*. Addison-Wesley, Reading, Massachusetts, 1978.

Pert, Candace B. The Wisdom of the Receptors. *Advances* 3:3, 8–16, 1986.

Rose, Colin. *Accelerated Learning*, 4th ed. Accelerated Learning Systems Ltd., Aylesbury, Bucks, England, 1989.

Sachs, Michael H. Exercise for Stress Control. *Mind/Body Medicine*. Daniel Goleman and Joel Gurin, eds. Consumer Reports Books, Yonkers, New York, 1993, pp. 315–327.

Schneider, Tom. *Everybody's a Winner: A Kid's Guide to New Sports and Fitness*. Little, Brown, Boston, 1976.

Shainberg, Lawrence. Finding the Zone. *New York Times Magazine*, April 9, 1989.

Sheehan, George. Basics of Jogging. *Runner's World*, vol. 12 (August 1977), p. 36 (in Murphy and White, *The Psychic Side of Sports*).

Smith, Fritz Frederick. *Inner Bridges: A Guide to Energy Movement and Body Structure*. Humanics New Age, Atlanta, 1990.

Todd, Mabel E. *The Thinking Body*. Dance Horizons, Inc. © 1937

Paul B. Hoeber, Inc., © 1949 Mabel E. Todd, and © 1959 Lulu E. Sweigard.

Welch, Martha G. *Holding Time*. Simon & Schuster, New York, 1988.

Chapter 6: Raising a Stress-Proof Child

Chess, Stella, and Thomas, Alexander. *Know Your Child: An Authoritative Guide for Today's Parents*. Basic Books, New York, 1987.

Cousins, Norman. *Anatomy of an Illness*. Norton, New York, 1979.

Cousins, Norman. *Head First: The Biology of Hope*. E. P. Dutton, New York, 1989.

Haggerty, Robert J. Behavioral Pediatrics: A Time for Research. *Pediatrics* 81(2):179–185, February 1988.

Holman, Halsted R. Arthritis. *How Your Mind Affects Your Health*. Institute for the Advancement of Health, San Francisco, 1990.

Maddi, Salvadore R., and Kobasa, Suzanne C. [Ouelette] *The Hardy Executive: Health Under Stress*. Dow Jones–Irwin, Homewood, Illinois, 1984.

McDaniel, Sandy, and Bielen, Peggy. *Project Self-Esteem: A Parent Involvement Program for Elementary-Age Children*. B. L. Winch & Associates, Rolling Hills Estates, California, 1986.

Mind-Body Education. *Mind-Body-Health Digest* 4:3, 1990.

Rich, Dorothy. *Megaskills*, revised & updated. Houghton Mifflin, New York, 1992.

Seligman, Martin E.P. *Learned Optimism*. Alfred A. Knopf, New York, 1991.

Trad, Paul V. *Psychosocial Scenarios for Pediatrics*. Springer-Verlag, New York, 1988.

Trad, Paul V. Stress and Child Development. *Advances* 6:4, 1989.

Tuttle, Cheryl, and Paquette, Penny. *Thinking Games to Play with Your Child*. Lowell House, Los Angeles, 1991.

Vernon, Ann. *Thinking, Feeling, Behaving: An Emotional Education Curriculum*. Research Press, Champaign, Illinois, 1989.

Weissberg, Roger P.; Caplan, Marlene; Bennetto, Loisa; and Jackson, Alice Stroup. *The Sixth Grade Social Problem-Solving Module* (1990–1991). Available from: Roger P. Weissberg, Ph.D., Department of Psychology, Box 11A, Yale Station, Yale University, New Haven, CT 06520-7447; (203) 432-4530.

Williams, Redford. *The Trusting Heart: Great News About Type A Behavior*, Chapter 9: "Let's Have More Trusting Children." Times Books, New York, 1989.

Wonder, Jacquelyn, and Donovan, Priscilla. *Whole-Brain Thinking: Working from Both Sides of the Brain to Achieve Peak Job Performance*. Quill & Co./William Morrow, New York, 1984.

Chapter 7: The Social Connection: Helping Your Child Get Along with Others

Berkman, Lisa F., and Syme, S. Leonard. Social Networks, Host Resistance, and Mortality: A Nine-Year Follow-up Study of Alameda County Residents. *American Journal of Epidemiology* 109 (1979):186–204.

Covey, Stephen R. *The Seven Habits of Highly Effective People: Powerful Lessons in Personal Change*. Fireside Books/Simon & Schuster, New York, 1989.

Curran, Dolores. *Traits of a Healthy Family*. Winston Press, Minneapolis, 1983.

Edelman, Marian Wright. "Kids First!" *Mother Jones* 16:3, May–June 1991. Published by Foundation for National Progress, San Francisco, p. 31.

Growald, Eileen Rockefeller, and Luks, Allan. Beyond Self. *American Health*. March 1988, p. 51.

Health Benefits of Helping. Conclusions of a June 1988 Conference, Institute for the Advancement of Health, New York, 1988.

Heschel, Abraham Joshua. *God in Search of Man.* Farrar, Straus & Giroux, New York, 1976.

Keirsey, David, and Bates, Marilyn. *Please Understand Me: Character and Temperament Types.* Prometheus Nemesis Book Co., Del Mar, California, 1978.

Luks, Allan, with Payne, Peggy. *The Healing Power of Doing Good.* Ballantine Books, New York, 1991.

Mind-Body Education. *Mind-Body-Health Digest* 4:3, 1990.

The Mysteries Sourcebook. Crossroads School, Santa Monica, California.

Ornish, Dean. *Dr. Dean Ornish's Program for Reversing Heart Disease.* Random House, New York, 1990.

Chapter 8: Taking a Hero's Journey

Boorstin, Daniel J. *The Creators: A History of Heroes of the Imagination.* Vintage Books, New York, 1992.

Campbell, Joseph. *The Hero with a Thousand Faces.* Princeton University Press, Princeton, New Jersey, 1972.

Cardoso, Pamela. *Special Friends. Exceptional Parent* 21:7, October/November 1991.

Pearson, Carol S. *Awakening the Heroes Within: Twelve Archetypes to Help Us Find Ourselves and Transform Our World.* HarperCollins Publishers, San Francisco, 1991.

Pearson, Carol S. *The Hero Within: Six Archetypes We Live By.* HarperCollins Publishers, New York, 1989.

Chapter 9: Special Situations

Cautela, Joseph R., and Groden, June. *Relaxation: A Comprehen-*

sive Manual for Adults, Children, and Children with Special Needs. Research Press Company, Champaign, Illinois, 1978.

Chaney, Sky, and Fisher, Pam, eds. *The Discovery Book: A Helpful Guide for the World Written by Children with Disabilities*, revised edition. United Cerebral Palsy of the North Bay, Santa Rosa, California, 1989.

Donovan, Denis M., and McIntyre, Deborah. *Healing the Hurt Child: A Developmental-Contextual Approach*. Norton, New York, 1990.

Elliott, Charles H., and Olson, Roberta A. The Management of Children's Distress in Response to Painful Medical Treatment for Burn Injuries. *Behaviour Research and Therapy* 21 (6):675–83, 1983.

Fernald, C.D., and Corry, J.J. Empathetic versus directive preparation of children for needles. *Journal of the Association for the Care of Children's Health* 10:44–47, 1981.

Fine, Judylaine. *Afraid to Ask: A Book for Families to Share About Cancer*. Lothrop, Lee & Shepard Books, New York, 1986.

Gaes, Jason. *My book for kids with cansur: A Child's Autobiography of Hope*, illustrated by Tim and Adam Gaes. Melius & Peterson Publishing, Aberdeen, South Dakota, 1987.

Gershwin, M. Eric, and Klingelhofer, Edwin. *Conquering Your Child's Allergies*. Addison-Wesley, Reading, Massachusetts, 1989.

Hunsberger, Mabel; Love, Barbara; Byrne, Carolyn. A Review of Current Approaches Used to Help Children and Parents Cope with Health Care Procedures. *Maternal-Child Nursing Journal* 13 (3):145–65, Fall 1984.

Johnson, Kendall. *Trauma in the Lives of Children: Crisis and Stress Management Techniques for Teachers, Counselors, and Student Service Professionals*. Hunter House, Claremont, California, 1989.

Lobato, Debra J. *Brothers, Sisters, and Special Needs. Information and Activities for Helping Young Siblings with Chronic Illnesses and Developmental Disabilities.* Paul H. Brookes Pub. Co., Baltimore, Maryland, 1990.

Mack, Alison. *Dry All Night: The Picture Book Technique That Stops Bedwetting.* Little, Brown, Boston, Massachusetts, 1989.

Marley, Linda S. The Use of Music with Hospitalized Infants and Toddlers: A Descriptive Study. *Journal of Music Therapy* 21(3):126–32, Fall 1984.

Mind-Body-Health Digest 3:1. Institute for the Advancement of Health, San Francisco, 1989.

Olness, K., MacDonald, J.T., and Uden, D.L. Comparison of Self-Hypnosis and Propranolol in the Treatment of Juvenile Classic Migraine. *Pediatrics* 79:593–97, 1987.

Peterson, Lizette, and Harbeck, Cynthia. *The Pediatric Psychologist: Issues in Professional Development and Practice.* Research Press, Champaign, Illinois, 1988.

Peterson, L., and Shigetomi, C. The Use of Coping Techniques to Minimize Anxiety in Hospitalized Children. *Behavior Therapy* 12:1–4, 1981.

Peterson, L., and Shigetomi, C. One-year Follow-up of Elective Surgery Child Patients Receiving Preoperative Preparation. *Journal of Pediatric Psychology* 7:43–48, 1982.

Pilkington, Rosemarie. Cyberphysiology in Children. *Advances* 5(4):66–69, 1988.

Porter, Garrett, and Norris, Patricia. *Why Me? Harnessing the Healing Power of the Human Spirit.* Stillpoint Publishing, Walpole, New Hampshire, 1985.

Poster, Elizabeth C. Stress Immunization: Techniques to Help Children Cope with Hospitalization. *Maternal-Child Nursing Journal* 12:119–34, Summer 1983.

Terr, Lenore C. Chowchilla Revisited: The Effects of Psychic Trauma Four Years After a School-Bus Kidnapping. *American Journal of Psychiatry* 140:1543–1550, 1983.

Trad, Paul V. *Psychosocial Scenarios for Pediatrics*. Springer-Verlag, New York, 1988.

Acknowledgments

We are grateful to many children and adults for their generosity of spirit, wisdom, and time in the preparation of this book. (We regret any omissions or errors.)

Our thanks to the many children who first tried out the exercises; shared their thoughts, feelings, and concerns with us; posed for the illustrations and contributed their creative writing and illustrations. A special thanks to Anya, Eric, Hannah Grace, Gregory, Jamie, Jeremy, Jessie, Sarah G., Sarah K., Margie, Matthew, Natasha, Ilan, Tavor, Jessica, Benjamin, Anna, Marty, Jennifer, Patrick, Kyle, Shana, and our nieces and nephews, especially Heather, Sasha, Rami, and Sivan, their parents, and all our siblings. And most of all, we thank our two sons, Ezra and Zachary, for sharing, posing, experimenting, and nudging this book—and us—forward in countless ways.

We are indebted to the pioneers in mind-body practices with children and holistic education for sharing their stories, wisdom, and experience. They include:

Suzanne Abeloff, of the Parkside School; Ivan Barzakov, founder of OptimaLearning®, Cinda Fisher, and Leo Wood;

Herbert Benson, founding president of the Mind-Body Medical Institute and Chief of Behavioral Medicine at New England Deaconess Hospital and Margaret Ennis of the Mind-Body Institute; Sasha Borenstein (learning disabilities specialist and "positive learning" advocate) of the Kelter Center in Los Angeles; Carolyn Brown, of the Commonweal Children's Program in Bolinas, California; Bonnie Bainbridge Cohen, of the School for Body-Mind Centering in Amherst; Bobbi DePorter, of Super-Camp and author of *Quantum Learning*; Moshe Elbaum, of Body Balance Institute in Israel; Karol DiFalco, of the New Haven Social Development Project; Tiffany Field, of the Touch Research Institute at the University of Miami; Donna Steer Friedman, special educator in Nashville; June Groden, of the Groden Center in Providence; Lois Holzman, of Empire State College (of S.U.N.Y.) and director of the Barbara Taylor School; Marilyn Howell, of Brookline High School; childbirth and family educator Sandy Jamrog; Shelley Kessler, a pioneer in social and emotional learning who developed the Mysteries program; Daniel P. Kohen, of the Behavioral Pediatrics Program, University of Minnesota; Leora Kuttner, of the Vancouver Children's Hospital; Christine La Cerva, of the Family Development Center at the East Side Institute; Linda Lantieri, of Resolving Conflict Creatively Program; Josette and Sambhava Luvmour of Pathfinders/Center for Educational Guidance; Nancy Margulies, author, illustrator, and educator; Ann Meyers, of the Manhattan Beach school system; Reed Moskowitz, founder and medical director of the Stress Disorders Medical Services Program of New York University; Maureen Murdock, author of *Spinning Inward*; Barbara Neiman, occupational therapist; Diane Nichols, of Miller Health Care Institute for Performing Artists; Suzanne C. Ouelette, of the City University of New York; Carol Perry, of the Trinity School in Manhattan; Lizette Peterson, of the University of Missouri at Columbia; Amy Pivar and Freda Rosen, choreographers; Otto Rand, of R.E.A.L. Education; William Redd, of Memorial Sloan-Kettering Cancer Center; Roger Weissberg, of the University of Illinois at Chicago; Joyce Robinson, of the Quest Program at the Dwight School; Janice Rous, breath and movement specialist; Mike and Nancy Samuels, authors of *The Well Child Book*; Stephen Spahn, chan-

cellor of the Dwight School; Suzi Tortora-Biederman, movement therapist; Livia Vanaver, of the Vanaver Caravan; Ann Vernon, of the University of Northern Iowa in Cedar Falls; Charlene Voyce, coordinator of the Collaborative for the Advancement of Social and Emotional Learning at the Yale Child Study Center; Kathleen Walker, physical education specialist; Judith Waller-stein, of the Center for the Family in Transition; Mary Beth Weinstock, dance therapist.

Our appreciation to the American Academy for Child and Adolescent Psychiatry, for their permission to use material from the Facts for Families series; the Association for the Care of Children's Health; to Debra Babcock, Mary Reilly, Nancy Adler, Stephanie Endler, and Nina Patella for sharing with us their expertise on hatha yoga exercises; to the students and staff—Andre, Angela, Caryn, and Pat—of the Barbara Taylor School; to the participants, in the work of the Family Development Center at the East Side Institute—including Christine La Cerva, Bette Braun, Fred Newman, Hugh Polk, Lew Steinhardt, Deborah Ifel, Lois Holzman, Barbara Taylor, and Debra Pearl; Zach, Kaya, Alana, Amy, Mark, Matthew; Kim, Diane, Cara, Maria, Raul, and the Tuesday group.

We wish to thank Eileen Rockefeller Growald, founder of the Institute for the Advancement of Health (IAH), for her contributions to the fields of mind-body health and social/emotional learning and for granting us permission to quote from *Advances* and *Mind-Body-Health Digest*; James A. Autry, with whom we feel a special bond, who is a tireless advocate for all children, particularly those with special needs; Allan Luks, executive director of Big Brothers/Big Sisters of New York; Judy Johns, Maria Norris, Lisa Wood, Diane Cramer, Gilles Mesrobian, Sandra Harris, and Gerry Goodman.

Advances, the Journal of Mind-Body Health (now published by the John E. Fetzer Institute) is once again in the able hands of its founding editor, Harris Dienstfrey. *Advances* continues to be a great source of information and ideas to us and others interested in the mind-body field.

We have been profoundly influenced by the work and words of many of the leading researchers and clinicians in mind-body medicine. They include:

Robert Ader, Herbert Benson, Joan Borysenko, Deepak Chopra, Larry Dossey, Joel Elkes, Bernard H. Fox, Jimmie C. Holland, Steven E. Locke, Neal Miller, Brendan O'Regan, Dean Ornish, Kenneth R. Pelletier, Rachel Naomi Remen, Martin L. Rossman, Jon Kabat-Zinn, and Mady Hornig-Rohan. A special mention to Michael Lerner, president of Commonweal, for his commitment to the needs and development of young people.

To trailblazing editors and writers in the mind-body field: Harris Dienstfrey, T. George Harris, Daniel Goleman, Joel Gurin, Martin Edelston, and the late Norman Cousins, who encouraged us to write this book.

This project came into being through conversations with Joan Borysenko about the need for a mind-body health book for parents and children. We thank Joan for her inspiration, example, and support.

Much has been made of the connection between social support and health. We would like to express our appreciation to the many friends and colleagues who make up our social support system, especially:

Barbara Graham (first and foremost), Georgi and Robert Antar, Marc and Susan Black, Richard Caccione, Margarita Danielian, Hugh Delehanty, Mary Gartner, Kathleen and Paul Ellis, Susan and Marty Goldstein, Joy Harris Kevin Hart, Amy Hertz, Miriam Kaplan, Ken and Barbara Klaristenfeld, Ed and Denny Levy, Edward Levy, Stuart and Gitesha Marmorstein, the Morningstars, Pamela Miles, Kathleen and Paul Mlotok, Barbara Neiman, Mirtha Quintanales, Ruth and Mario, Sue Sencer, Sherie Senné, Lew S., Sheila Tucker, Judith Tumin, Carolyn Vaughn, Baylah Wolf, Bette Ziegler, the Whites, the Zaitchiks, and the Kaufmans.

Special thanks to our hands-on team: David Celsi for his wonderful illustrations (and to Mary Ann Nichols for helping us find David); Margarita Danielian, for manuscript preparation, technical support, and constructive criticism; Ronnie Kaufman, for her help designing the charts and her endless encouragement; and the readers of early drafts, including Margaret Ennis and Patti Hayes.

To our editors: Leslie Meredith, for her guidance and careful

shaping of the manuscript during its early stages; Brian Tart, for his organizational talent, enthusiasm, and grace under pressure; Toni Burbank, Linda Gross, and the rest of the Bantam staff for their support and helpful comments.

To our agent, Ann Rittenberg, for her kind heart, sharp eye, quick wit, and heroic patience.

We are deeply grateful to our meditation teacher, Swami Chidvilasananda, for sharing with us the ancient—yet amazingly contemporary and universal—practices and teachings of Siddha yoga meditation. They continuously uplift our experience of family life.

And finally, we again thank our children and parents. We couldn't have done it without you.

About the Authors

Sheldon Lewis is a journalist specializing in psychological aspects of health and illness. He was director of publications at the Institute for the Advancement of Health (which was devoted to the study of mind-body interactions), where he was editor of *Advances, the Journal of Mind-Body Health,* and the newsletter *Mind-Body-Health Digest.*

He is a former senior editor of the newsletters *Health Confidential* and *Bottom Line/Personal.* He was a member of the editorial staff of *Scientific American Medicine,* a loose-leaf medical textbook for physicians, published by Scientific American. His articles on health and medicine have appeared in *Longevity, Medical Dimensions, Bottom Line/Personal, Health Confidential,* and other publications.

He is currently writing a book on emotions and cancer with Dr. Jimmie C. Holland, chief of psychiatry at Memorial Sloan-Kettering Cancer Center, with whom he wrote the chapter on cancer for the book *Mind-Body Medicine* (Consumer Reports Press, 1993).

Sheila Kay Lewis is a longtime educator and writer, with a special interest in holistic education—that is, learning with the

whole body and mind: thinking, feeling, interacting, doing, and moving through multisensory activities.

She has led enrichment programs, teaching hundreds of children art, study skills, and mind-body techniques such as yoga, relaxation and visualization.

As former vice president of R.E.A.L. Education, Inc., she designed and implemented a holistic-education curriculum for New York City school teachers and students. She taught study skills to high school students at the Dwight School in Manhattan, and to private students. She is a program specialist for the Girl Scouts of America national headquarters in New York City, where she writes program materials and trains Girl Scout leaders in using them.

For many years, she was educational director of a holistic health center in New York City, where she developed training manuals for health professionals and designed courses in yoga, massage, nutrition, and mind-body techniques.

Her articles and stories have appeared in *Highlights, Welcome Home, Parents League Newsletter, Naissance*, and other publications for parents and children.

She holds a master's degree in educational media and technology from Columbia University, Teachers College, and a bachelor of fine arts from Boston University.

The Lewises have two sons, Ezra and Zachary.